TONY OYATEDOR

THANKS BE TO THE CREATOR WITHOUT WHOSE HELP NOTHING IS POSSIBLE. PRAISE BE TO ALMIGHTY GOD/ALLAH.

LEADERSHIP

BY

TONY OYATEDOR

Leadership
by Tony Oyatedor
MOUNT HELICON PRESS

Address comments and inquiries to:
MOUNT HELICON PRESS
American Publishing Service
9710 Traville Gateway Drive, #305,
Rockville, MD 20850

E-mail:
jrock@mountheliconpress.com   lrock@mountheliconpress.com
Internet URL: www.mountheliconpress.com

Hardback ISBN: 1-59663-751-x

Printed in the United States of America

First published 1995

This printing June 2005

This book is dedicated to my wife,
Mrs. Veronica Okosun Oyatedor

To my children
Tony Tijani Oyatedor, Jr. Irene Amina Oyatedor,
Stefanie Zainab Oyatedor, Kevina Alima Oyatedor and
Kevin Clinton Ibrahim Oyatedor,
my greatest supporters.

To my brothers
Bernard, Peter, Kent and John

To my sisters
Mrs. Beauty Ekadi, Ebikaboere,
Comfort, Joy, and Hope Oyatedor

To my loving parents
Chief Felix Disi Oyatedor and
Mrs. Lucy Kentebe Oyatedor
*with love and appreciation for all
they have given me*

To the loving memory of my father and mother

MR. TONY OYATEDOR WITH
PROFESSOR JIBRIL AMINU —
PROMINENT EDUCATOR IN NIGERIA.

The objective of this book is
to inform and to inspire.

CHANGING NIGERIA STARTS
WITH YOU --- TAKE
THE FIRST STEP, DO NOT WAIT
FOR SOMEONE ELSE.

THE AUTHOR, MR. TONY OYATEDOR, WITH ACTING
CHIEF OF NAVAL STAFF OF THE NIGERIAN NAVY,
REAR ADMIRAL O. P. FINGESI, DURING AN
INSPECTION TOUR OF WESTERN NAVAL COMMAND
IN APAPA LAGOS, NIGERIA.

CONTENTS

ACKNOWLEDGMENTS

I would like to acknowledge my gratitude and eternal debt to Alhaji Mamman Nassarawa, Retired Assistant Inspector General of Police; late Alhaji Saminu Duara, Deputy Inspector General of Police; Alhaji Muhammadu Gambo, Inspector General of Police; Admiral Muritala Nyako, Retired Chief of Naval Staff; Chief Andy Akporugo, Managing Director, African Guardian magazine; Admiral Festus Porbeni; Major General John Shagaya; Chief Ebitimi E. Banigo; Chief Gani Fawehenmi; Chief Ben Murray-Bruce, Managing Director, Silverbird Productions; Chief Uzor Kalu; Professor Jibril Aminu; Dr. Ephraim Okoro, Ph.D., Secretary of the Board of Trustees, South Eastern University, Washington, DC, United States of America; Chief Nuel Ojei, Managing Director, Nuel Holdings; Rear Admiral O. P. Fingesi, Retired Officer, commanding Western Naval Command; Alhaji Garba Gumel, Managing Director, Nigeria Hotels, Limited; late Navy Commodore Edwin Kentebe; Pa. G. M.; Otubu, Head of Eternal Sacred Order of Cherubim and Seraphim; Chief Sam Amuka, Publisher Vanguard newspaper; Pa and Mrs. D. A. Okosun; Alhaji Abubakar Musa, Retired Director of Customs; Alozie Ogugbuaja, Police Public Relations Officer, Lagos State command; Nduka Obaigbena, Publisher, This Week magazine; Chief Willy Bozimo, Retired Deputy General Manager, News Agency of Nigeria (NAN); Dr. Charles Adeoye; Chief Sunny Kentebe, Retired General Manager Nitel; Dr. Ibrahim Tahir; Chief Sonny Okosun, world-famous musician; Isaiah Gowon, Retired Army Captain; Mr. Thomas Pickering, United States Ambassador to Nigeria; Mr. John Bennett, Counsel General United States Embassy, Lagos, Nigeria; Mr. David Finger, computer expert in Washington, DC, United States of America; Chief M.K.O. Abiola, General Olusegun Obasanjo; and others too numerous to mention

Finally, I would like to thank my wife, Mrs. Veronica Okosun Oyatedor, whose advice and enthusiastic support sustained me through the long and occasionally daunting process of completing this book.

THE AUTHOR, MR. TONY OYATEDOR, WITH
FORMER NIGERIAN MILITARY HEAD-OF-STATE,
GENERAL OLUSEGUN OBASANJO.

PREFACE

This is the essential Nigerian story. In order to tell it, one has to live it, one has to acquire the skill of telling the story and the perspective to see it whole. TONY OYATEDOR has done all these and more.

This is an exhilarating book.

DR. EPHRAIM OKORO, Ph.D.
Howard University, Washington, D.C.

NIGERIA'S FUTURE?
WHO KNOWS, BUT IDEAS
KEEP EMERGING.

MR. TONY OYATEDOR WITH
CHIEF GANI FAWEHENMI—LAWYER AND
HUMAN RIGHTS ACTIVIST.

**TRUTH STANDS ALONE
IN THE CROWD OF LIES.**

TRANSITION SINCE INDEPENDENCE

Nigeria ------ Africa's most populous nation has been under military leadership for (as at the time of this writing, 1995) 25 of 35 years since she gained independence from Britain in 1960.

Population of the country: 102.2 million (1995 EST.)

Area: 356.669 square miles (it is twice the size of California State in the United States of America)

Ethnic make up: The country has more than 250 ethnic groups which includes Hausa/Fulani -- 30 percent, Yoruba -- 20 percent, Igbo -- 17 percent and Ijaw -- 9 percent.

Religion: Muslim -- 50 percent, Christian -- 45 percent and others -- 5 percent.
Major industries: Crude oil, food processing and vehicle assembly (not vehicle manufacturing).

G.D.P. per capita: Per capita income has fallen from $1,000.00 in 1980 to $300.00 in 1995.

Life expectancy: 54 years for men, 57 years for women.

Literacy: 61 percent.

SINCE INDEPENDENCE

October 1, 1960: Nigeria achieves independence from Britain. Alhaji Abubakar Tafawa Balewa becomes the first Prime Minister. Dr. Azikiwe becomes first ceremonial President.

January 15, 1966: Alhaji Abubakar Tafawa Balewa and some civilian leaders were killed in a military coup that brought the establishment of the first military government in the country under Major General Johnson Aguiyi-Ironsi (an Igbo indegene), this is also the first and only Igbo-led coup till date - 1995. Major General Aguiyi-Ironsi attempted to do away with the nation's four regions and establish a unitary state. This brought indignation in the Northern part of Nigeria, which is inhabited mostly by the Hausa/Fulani tribes.

July 29, 1966: Then Col. Yakubu Gowon -- (now a retired General) a Northerner, with the concerted assistance from the Yorubas, overthrows General Aguiyi-Ironsi's regime and thus established his own military government. This established the first Northern-led coup and it has not stopped since then to date 1995, General Yakubu Gowon then reorganized the former four regions into 12 states.

May 30, 1967: Then Col. Odumegbu Ojukwu, dissatisfied with the central government led by General Yakubu Gowon whom Ojukwu perceived as not only a junior-ranked officer but also felt General Yakubu Gowon had a vendetta against the Igbos for the killings of Northerners during the Aguiyi-Ironsi administration. The mostly Igbo eastern region declares itself the independent Republic of Biafra in response to General Yakubu Gowon's attempt at reorganization. The Ijaws and the Calabars in the eastern region refused to join the Biafra Republic instead opted to remain with the federal

Republic of Nigeria.

The federal military government of Nigeria under the leadership of General Yakubu Gowon refused to recognize the secession of the Republic of Biafra, subsequently hostilities break out on July 6, 1967.

January 15, 1970: (one day after my mother's death - January 14th 1970). After a protracted civil war that claimed an estimate 1.5 million lives on both sides, the Biafran rebels surrendered to Nigeria.

July 29, 1975: In a bloodless coup, General Yakubu Gowon was overthrown by General Murtala Ramat Muhammad. In October of the same year along with his Chief of staff, General Olusegun Obasanjo creates a commission to draft a new constitution that would return Nigeria to a civilian rule.

February 13, 1976: General Murtala Ramat Muhammad was assassinated in an unsuccessful coup attempt led by Lt.Col. Buka Suka Dimka. General Olusegun Obasanjo assumes leadership of the federal military government.

September 12, 1978: Twelve-year-old acute state of emergency was lifted, ban on all political parties and political activities was rescinded.

July 1979: Elections were held for federal senators and house of representatives.

August 11, 1979: Nigeria's first civilian leader since 1966, Alhaji Shehu Usman Aliyu Shagari was elected President of the federal Republic of Nigeria.

December 31, 1983: I was in Nigerian Television

3

Authority (N.T.A. network-news newsroom) with other fellow journalists when we were jolted by news flash on the radio that senior military officers including Major General Ibrahim Babangida and the man who made the announcement on the radio, then Brigadier Sanni Abacha overthrew the civilian elected government of President Shagari. Few moments later, the entire offices of N.T.A. Victoria Island was overtaken by military officers. Later Major General Muhammadu Buhari was installed as Nigeria's new military ruler.

August 27, 1985: General Muhammadu Buhari and his so-called strong man Major General Tunde Idiagbon, a man who never smiled when he was a Brigadier and started showing some teeth and fervent smiling face right after he was promoted Major General because he was aware if there was a coup while he was a Brigadier he will not receive retirement money but as a Major General whatever happens he will receive retirement funds for the rest of his life. They were deposed by members of the supreme Military Council and middle-ranked soldiers. Major General Ibrahim Badamasi Babangida, was announced as President of the Federal Military government.

September 1987: General Ibrahim Badamasi Babangida begins what he calls the beginning of the end of military rule in Nigeria, he starts the transition to civilian rule that will end in 1990 and bring about military disengagement in the political life of Nigeria. The target date of 1990 was eventually shifted to 1992, then to 1993, then to 1994. All former politicians were banned from seeking any political office and the ban was later lifted in 1991.

December 12, 1987: Local Government elections were held. A vast majority of them were ruled invalid.

May 1989: The ban on all political parties and political activities were lifted. To the repulsive and amazement of the federal military government thirteen political parties vie for registration with the federal military government. The IBB-led junta rejects them due to ambiguity and other reasons and eventually creates two official government-inspired parties --- (Social Democratic Party S.D.P., and National Republican Party N.R.C.) to compete in local government elections on December 8, 1990.

December 1991: Elections were held for state governorships and seats in state legislatures.

July 4, 1992: National Assembly elections were held.

August 7, 1992: Presidential primaries were held, but the federal military government under the leadership of Ibrahim Badamasi Babangida disallows the results. New presidential primaries were held in September of the same year (1992) these primaries too were nullified and all the entire participants were barred from further political participation in elections till further notice.

June 12, 1993: The date of crucial importance to the political crisis that has engulfed Nigeria since independence. Despite legal challenges in some quarters and allegations of enormous fraud, the Presidential election was held with a repugnant turn out of just over 30 percent of the entire registered voters. Partial and somewhat ultimate returns indicated that Aare Ono Kakanfo Chief Moshood Kashimawo Abiola, a business man from Southwestern Nigeria -- a Yoruba and a Muslim, out polled his opponent Alhaji Bashir Tofa, a business man from the Northern part of Nigeria.

June 23, 1993: General Ibrahim Badamasi Badangida for some ominous reasons known to him and his Armed Forces

5

Ruling Council (A.F.R.C.) members nullifies the June 12 Presidential elections.

August 26, 1993: On the day before he originally promised and scheduled to hand over power to an elected civilian government with a civilian President , General Ibrahim Badamasi Babangida (often referred to as IBB) steps down from the presidential podium as President and installs a full military-backed interim government headed by (his hand-picked) business man Chief Shonekan, who hails from the same South-western part of Nigeria with the man whom every one thought should have assumed the position of President --- Chief M.K.O. Abiola, whose first three initials are referred to in many quarters in the country as M --for money , K --for Kudi (meaning money in Hausa) and O --for owo (meaning money in Yoruba).

September 10, 1993: Chief Shonekan's interim government schedules Presidential elections for February 1994.

November 17, 1993: General Sanni Abacha, who has been General Officer Commanding the 1st division (G.O.C.1) under General Muhammadu Buhari, Chief of Army Staff, Chairman Joint Chiefs of Staff and later Chief of Defense Staff under General Ibrahim Badamasi Babangida and Defense Minister under Shonekan's interim government, assumed power following a bloodless military coup. General Sanni Abacha on November 18th, 1993 dissolves all political parties, states and local government and federal legislatures. As at the time of writing this book (1995) General Sanni Abacha is still in power -- what a remarkable man.

A decent standard of living is not a fringe benefit, it is a fundamental debt that the federal government (military or politicians) owes the Nigerian people. Ideology is no longer

6

the issue, it is all about the quality of life. The people of Nigeria do not care if it is military or political leadership, all they ask for is compassionate leadership with a strong sense of purpose.

The drastic drop in the living standards of the people is devastating, both under military regimes and political administrations. The people are giving this warning --- if you are President or Head-of-state, you either lead or leave.

Millions of Nigerians are asking -- what in heavens name are we doing with the antiquated military/political systems that has not got the problems of Nigeria solved?

The nation needs calm and strong leadership that will crash through the barriers these systems have set up to keep Nigerians from expressing their opinions.

A true personification of leadership is a leader with honesty, integrity, duty to country, honor and high morality.

As leaders, most Chief of State in Nigeria do not seem to have displayed any intellectual curiosity, except in how to enrich their private bank accounts.

To the extent Nigeria succeeds or fail in her quest for economic recovery and prosperity, everything depends on Nigerians . It starts and ends with the will to succeed or fail.

Every single interest group that succeeds in the United States of America, it is due to the ability of coming together despite their social differences and social backgrounds and fighting for their people both at home and in the United States (e.g. the Arab league, the Italians, the Jewish league, the Irish etc.) just to name a few.

When will Southern Nigeria put envy aside and come together for the oneness and benefit of their people both in the United States of America and especially for their people in Nigeria? This is a crucial question that should be of utmost concern to Southern Nigerians.

TONY OYATEDOR IN A HAND-SHAKE WITH THE WINNER OF
THE PRESIDENTAL ELECTIONS IN NIGERIA, CHIEF M.K.O. ABIOLA

POLITICS IN NIGERIA

Before anyone can make informed conceptions about Nigerian politics, they should find out or know how it works. Politics anywhere in the world is not a matter of good people versus bad people. My objective here is to explain Nigerian politics as I saw and witnessed it under military and civilian administrations. I am not going to praise nor condemn any administration but I would try to explain them.

Politics is a prerequisite in any civilized society. Politics is unavoidable because people live together and because people have disparity in material desires and personal point of view.

Politics is unavoidable due to the fact that both <u>resources</u> and <u>power</u> must and should be shared in conformity to some kind of rule.

Politics is a way to express and resolve conflicts and differences. Politics is a way to organize people to do together what they would or could not do alone.

A great deal of politics consist of <u>bargaining</u> and <u>compromise</u> designed to give conflicting interests enough of what they want so that they will continue to cooperate with each other.

In Nigeria, there is no civilized bargaining or compromise to solve conflicting interests or group problem, <u>it is always my way or no way at all</u> hence you can not call it politics, you either call it political Autocracy or political dictatorship.

In politics, two or more groups each strongly backing its own candidate for office, may discover a third or fourth candidate whom they can all support with more enthusiasm than either had for their previous candidates.

To a large extent, whether a political system works depends on whether conflicts and interests can be broken down into small parts so that everyone can have something. If so, everyone will win sometimes and lose sometimes. This has been one of the principal challenges and stumbling blocks of Nigerian politics. The South claims that the North does not want to share the Presidency (or the office of Head-of-State, in the case of military regime), the North insists that the South has always been in the Presidency since independence, hence this is their turn (Northerners) for political leadership. With arguments like this going back and forth, it creates room for military intervention because each group or interest does not want to compromise. The North also claim that the South control the economy of Nigeria hence political power should be in the hands of Northerners.

The business sector i.e. banks, industries (both manufacturing and wholesale/retail) is controlled by the Igbos -- but the agricultural sector is controlled by the Hausa/Fulani. The oil sector which feeds the whole nation state of Nigeria is also controlled by the North or whomever is the President or Head-of-State.

The oil emanates from the Riverine areas of the South, yet these areas have no significant benefits accruing from the sale of oil, neither does her people thought of in the ramifications of leadership in the Nigerian political scene. Each time the discussions of political leadership is heightened, people only talk of three tribes in Nigeria, 1. the Hausa, 2. the Igbos and 3. The Yorubas, they forget entirely about the fourth largest tribe in Nigeria -- the Ijaws who also produces the wealth of the nation -- oil.

11

But you can not blame anybody but the Ijaws themselves. They do not have a political mouthpiece, the only newspaper produced by the Rivers State government "TIDE", is only circulated in Portharcourt the State capital. The other three major tribes, not only do they have nation wide circulated newspaper controlled by their various State governments they also have private ownership of newspapers, magazines and newsletters. Each of the big three also have money bags. As at the publication of this book, I am yet to see an Ijaw millionaire. One of the reason is that the big three, each uplift their fellow brothers and sisters but the Hausa/Fulani uplift themselves more than any other tribe thus the empowerment of the Northerners.

The Ijaws lack this empowerment due to greed, (the now syndrome, me and my family alone factor and most of all lack of togetherness). Sharing of power and resources should not be limited to the big three alone, the Ijaws should be encouraged and their people should uplift each other in order to achieve a better life for their community at large and the nation as a whole.

This region also has a common plight -- the Ijaws lack adequate housing, electricity, schools, employment opportunities, health services, transportation, commerce, political representation and other life sustaining basic amenities.

Most people in the oil-rich Ijaw region are fishermen or small-scale subsistence farmers. However, except for crude oil, the area is void of any growth industry.

The Ijaws face catastrophic health problems, they experience tremendously high incidences of death from preventable and most instances treatable diseases, high infant mortality rate and birth defects due to lack of adequate hospitals, clinics and trained medical/health personnel. Suitable rapid and reliable means of transportation are non-existent. Most houses are built with mud and are prey to heavy rainfall, floods, landslide erosion and natural disasters.

The exploitation of crude oil and natural gas led to the discharge of highly toxic substances into the air, soil and water. Besides long term health risks, these pollutants are also killing off fish and other marine life.

The traditional slace and burning method of farming and wasteful cutting down of trees in the forest have caused air pollution, erosion and also impacted on wildlife, hence depraving the people of their livelihood. All these combined has resulted in a chronic state of stagnation and underdevelopment. This state of underdevelopment exists despite the fact that the area is blessed with large amounts of crude oil and natural gas resources. The Ijaws have not derived any significant economic benefit from these resources.

In the United States of America, Texas state has the largest crude oil reserve in the U.S.A., hence this popular saying in Texas, "if you live a good life, say your prayer everyday when you die you go to Texas." This is a sign of confidence because the people of Texas feel and know that they are blessed with crude oil and that the sale and production of oil proceeds are used to beautify Texas hence they feel and know that Texas is heaven on earth.

One basic fact of politics is scarcity; many of the things people want do not exist in sufficient quantity to satisfy everybody. You can only have one President or Head-of-State. The South wants its candidate to be Head-of-State or President, the North wants the same thing but both are not willing to compromise, this and other situations leads to the

13

argument that Nigeria should not be a federation. The North is not happy with the South and vice versa.

Religion that has no place in politics has also ate deep down into the fabric of Nigerian politics. If you are not a Muslim, the North does not want you to be President, the South will also prefer you to be a Christian. Instead of thinking of themselves as Nigerians, regardless of the religion they belong to, the situation gives one region constant leadership role while the other region is a permanent loser. Because of the single Presidency, most candidates, forced themselves into office either through military coups or botched elections. There is not a single genuinely elected leader in Nigeria. They rig themselves into office. They either spend millions of Naira buying votes or they shoot their way through.

Candidates give village heads or traditional rulers Mercedes Benz cars in order for these people to influence their subjects for votes. These villagers or traditional leaders do not need a Mercedes Benz that they can not maintain, they need infrastructures to improve the quality of lives of their subjects, but due to selfish interests, the traditional rulers and the village leaders only know about themselves and their immediate family.

Nigerians need to educate themselves about thinking locally and acting globally, they need to think more about their communities, because if you think of your neighbor as a friend you feel safe and the only way to do that is to ensure that everyone in every community has the basic necessities of life.

Nigerians need to be educated in the art of uplifting each other to achieve the best in every one. In Nigerian politics, the South claims Northern domination in the scheme of political leadership, the North also claim that the South dominates the economic sphere. The Nigerian federation is suppose to be a secular state without any single religion dominating the others, but ironically the Muslim and Christian religions dominate the nation. The Northerners also do not see the Southern Muslim as a hard-core Muslim, because they insist that to be a true Muslim you must adopt Muhammedan names and Muhammedan culture.

As a secular state, the Nigerian government has no business with religion, neither should the government attempt to adopt one religion as the state religion.

Economic development will never take place in Nigeria, except jobs are created for the masses of Nigerians who are unemployed, most of them are university graduates.

Job restoration should be the hallmark of any administration, instead, every administration, that comes into power since General Yakubu Gowon's regime, always believe in mass retrenchment of workers thereby sending families who were once able to feed themselves into panic depression syndrome. Idle farmers in the rural areas and jobless city dwellers will welcome the commitment of any administration's fulfillment of job security and loans to harness the farms. The city dwellers and the rural farmers have had to bear most of the disproportionate burden of the economic situation in Nigeria. Jobs are decreasing while the population is increasing.

If people are going to invest their money in Nigeria, these people need some type of reassurance of political stability. African Americans and other U.S. indegenes would love to invest in Nigeria due to the large population of the country (Nigeria being the most populated Black nation on earth) but political instability is eroding the confidence of U.S. and

Japanese investors from investing in Nigeria. It is now up to any administration in power to revive the economy and help mend the bridge between the populace and government, the only way to do that is by putting the interest of the Nigerian people first.

Every administration has always claim that they put Nigeria's interest first whereas all of them, instead, have always put the interest of their own state and local areas first.

Until every leader in Nigeria put the interest of the people at large first (regardless of what part of Nigeria you are from) the system will be plodding the wrong way and drift aimlessly. I believe that things will get better when everybody start thinking of Nigerian community at large instead of thinking of selfish interests, I know things like this take time to develop, but we have to start from somewhere.

Money should be spend towards reducing the jobless rate in all sectors, you can not have some people from some part of the country constantly happy and the rest permanently in sorrow.

To facilitate peaceful co-existence, people should have jobs so as to feed themselves. Agricultural jobs should be created in every part of the country not just a certain part, manufacturing jobs should be created in every part of the country not just a certain part of the country.

The poor will remain in a stagnant slum of permanent poverty, if education and employment opportunities are neglected in any shape or form. Permanent illiteracy keeps people outside the realm of politics. Constant aid for education, job creation, agriculture and welfare would uplift the spirit of the Nigerian citizenry.

Any administration that builds the consensus needed to ensure a stable business environment is welcomed. To ensure this also, the administration needs tolerance of the opposition, the opposition also should give legitimate advice not incite people against any administration.

The media should not be muddled for every little report it writes against or that is not in good taste to the administration. The administration should seek redress on any false media allegation, but if these allegations are true the administration should be bold enough to take corrective measures, if possible, apologize to the populace.

Every arbitrary closure of media organization gives credence to any allegation and makes hundreds of workers stay home without a regular pay check and do not forget, most of these workers are not just journalist, you have drivers, typists, messengers etc. hence the saying "an hungry man is an angry man" is apt.

Agricultural development should be emphasized at all levels and sectors of the nation. Any nation that can feed itself and give her citizen jobs, is a powerful nation. Because a citizen who eats well would think well, study well, produce well and most of all make the nation and its immediate community proud.

Any administration that can put food on the table of every Nigerian, regardless of tribe and ensure job security would have made a valuable contribution to the history of Nigeria and her people and the world at large would forever remember and respect the leadership of such an administration.

In the U.S.A., people come to the Presidency with hope of being remembered for the good they did for the nation after they have left office, in Nigeria most leaders are always remembered for atrocities they committed to the treasury and the blatant killings of their so-called opponents, their wive's first boyfriend, their girlfriend's fiancé, their subordinates, their friends and sometimes family member who oppose them.

People in the United States Of America are happy despite their diversity, ethnicity, nationality, origin or creed. In the U.S.A. They say "the bigger the better", but a country like Nigeria (which is way smaller than the United States Of America), some people in the South are questioning the basis of Nigerian unity and they are clamoring for the breaking-up of Nigeria into bits and pieces. Now I ask, if you break-up Nigeria where would the Ijaws fit in? Apparently you will expect them to be in the Eastern region, but the Rivers people have vowed that they will rather die than to be colonized once again by the Igbos.

Most of the other ethnic groups like the TIVS do not want to stay in the North and be dominated by the Hausa/Fulani ethnic groups hence the country is better off the way it is but people (Africans generally) have to learn how to share power.

When people share power they feel they have a stake in the booty, hence the society will be safe, people will feel happier, they will not be eager for the break-up of Nigeria.

The Northerners are said to be holding their grips on power, the North is accused of not allowing the Igbos or Yorubas to gain leadership, but wait a minute, we have other ethnic groups, what about the Ijaws, the Bini, Isoko, Tiv etc. If the North wont allow the Yoruba nor the Igbo to leadership position then the other ethnic groups are available, or these people do not belong to leadership positions in Nigeria?

We have promising and eligible leaders from these other ethnic groups. Any group of people from any region of Nigeria who can not aspire to the position of leadership can not be expected to die for Nigeria.

In every administration in Nigeria instead of fighting the number one problem of the country which is <u>poverty</u>, administration officials are busy fighting for their own selfish needs. The North claims they have been marginalized, now the Southerners say they are being marginalized. Instead of people striving for the benefit of the country as <u>one</u>, they are busy regionalizing everything.

What most civilized nations believe is that every generation should strive to improve the living conditions of the next generation, but not in Nigeria, where every generation makes things worse for the generation after them.

Poverty is very much in the increase in Nigeria, you begin to wonder why is there a government at all. Crime is on the rise, because people do not have jobs, people do not know what to expect the next day, there is constant price increase on every consumable item, the government just sits around and watch. If people have jobs to pay for these items it is a very different scenario.

The so-called big-three major tribes (the Yoruba, the Igbo and Hausa) under President Shehu Shagari's administration proposed zoning the position of Presidency amongst themselves, forgetting the other ethnic groups including the fourth largest tribe in Nigeria -- the Ijaws.

Some sector of Nigerians criticize the federal character issue, but if you look at it closely the Northerners only want to be inclusive in every sector where they are lacking something hence the southerners should fight for inclusion for every sector that they feel they are lacking something.

A lot of politics consists of inventing ways for people with conflicting values or basic beliefs to live together. One would hope and pray that Nigerians will learn how to live together in peace. Especially by helping each other regardless of where you are from.

Politics itself is a major source of conflict, how you manage the conflict to the benefit of everybody is the real deal and the real inspiration that brings people together.

One of the things that politics is about is who shall govern. The earlier Nigerians learn how to share governance the better it will be for everybody. Without mechanisms for sharing and transferring of power (leadership), conflicts can result in revolution and or civil war.

One of the things that reduces tension in American politics (unlike in Nigeria) is the major fact that the losing political party knows definitely that it will get another chance in the next election . The rotation of political offices and officers among politicians is a major way of reducing the conflict that arises from politics itself. If Nigerian leaders are willing to share power they will not be in the quagmire they are in starting from President Shehu Shagari's time till present.

Activities aimed at improving the quality of life should not mean government ownership or operation, for instance, in the United States, the people (the citizens) pay for the planes and warship that defends the United States through taxes but most of the planes and warships are built in private factories.

For government to be effective, political parties and administration officials must expend a great deal of energy collectively on internal processes on making government work for the citizenry.

Although, not all politicians or civil servants are good public servants, some of them are but not in high numbers, encouragement should be given to those who work for the benefit of Nigeria and their immediate environs. Some politicians and administration officials however, are self-serving and this is in the high numbers starting from the regime of the late General Murtala Ramat Muhammed, during his time, people found out that they were being dismissed "with immediate effect" from the radio, without regards for future plans nor rehabilitation. Since then, most self-serving politicians or administration officials started planning for the future immediately they get into office because they feel they do not know tomorrow they might as well take what they can today and let tomorrow take care of itself, they were not going to wait to be dismissed "with immediate effect" without grabbing something for themselves for the future. Nation-serving became a thing of the past. Leaders today must insist that nation-serving comes first before anything.

Self- interest is one of the basic fuels of politics. This self-interest does not mean personal interest but community interest and nation's interest. One of the major purpose of politics is the art of getting people to work together to solve their problems, until the South and the North start to solve their problems together amicably and peacefully, things will definitely deteriorate to an all time low.

Politics is also a mixture of desire for self-advancement (not necessarily in monetary terms) and an innate desire to do good. The art of politics involves compromise (but not in Nigeria -- in Nigeria, rigidity or dictatorship is the in-thing). Political compromise is built on giving everybody something and treating everybody with equality. Political skill is a skill at risking and channeling conflict at accepting some risk and hostility in order to achieve goals. May be it is time for Nigerian men to try Nigerian women to do something in politics because so far, the men are just saying things and not doing things effectively, compassionately and or properly.

A politician should know when and whom to fight, when and which direction to run and to move people. This brings to the point of my friends -- Chief M.K.O. Abiola and General Sanni Abacha, not only did Abiola did not know whom and when to fight, he also did not know what direction to run and move people. In the first instance, before declaring himself President under a new military regime was undermining the power of the sitting military regime, he Abiola knows that when the Buhari regime took over power from President Shehu Shagari, nobody in President Shagari's administration went anywhere to declare themselves still in power, also when Babangida took over power from Buhari, nobody in Buhari's administration declared themselves as still in power, even the so-called "strong man" Major General Tunde Idiagbon never returned from Mecca to face the Babangida administration and declare himself strong man of the Buhari administration, instead he went hiding in his home state of Kwara, quietly because he had been retired "with immediate effect" by the sitting Babangida administration, hence Chief Abiola should not have declared himself President under the Abacha regime even if he thinks the administration was a continuation of the Babangida regime; but in all fairness, it was not Abacha who canceled the Abiola-led victory election, it was Babangida who annulled the elections, hence the right time and the right person Chief Abiola should have picked a fight with was Babangida and the only time Chief Abiola should have declared himself President due to the obvious victory was when Babangida continued his rulership and handed over power to Shonekan, a lot of people including the military would have supported him and he would have a legitimate reason to do so. Also where to run and people to move, Chief Abiola should have a substantial backing from some sector of the military (at least a large majority) before declaring himself President.

Another friend of mine who did not know when and whom to fight and how to cut his loss and run was the late Chief Obafemi Awolowo, in the 1979 campaign/elections, he was asked what will he do about the corrupt situation of the military, Chief Awolowo bluntly revealed (without any diplomacy) that he will probe the military. When top military brass heard this statements, of course they ensured that the Presidency was not handed over to Chief Awolowo. Another case-in-point was during the 1983 campaign/elections, at the Unity Party of Nigeria (U.P.N.) convention at the National Arts Theater in Iganmu Lagos, the Northerners and the Igbo's in the South were expecting that Chief Awolowo would step down as the U.P.N national flag bearer and nominate the more liberal, pragmatic and centrist -- Alhaji Lateef Jakande, instead there was no form of democracy at the convention because Chief Awolowo, due to his own self interest announced that all the sitting U.P.N governors were not to be challenged by their deputies or from any other quarters and that Chief Awolowo was still going to be the flag bearer of the U.P.N, you the reader should have been there to see the turmoil that ensued after his (chief Awolowo's) speech, be that as it may, this is how people started leaving the U.P.N and this gave the National Party of Nigeria (N.P.N) a better ground to fish for one of Chief Awolowo's utmost loyalists, Chief Akin Omoboriowo (better known as Owoboriomo) who joined the N.P.N with all the known secrets of Chief Awolowo and specially his campaign and electioneering style and stick it right in the ears of the N.P.N chieftains who used this and counter all of Chief Awolowo's plans, that was why the N.P.N could claim such a big landslide victory at the 1983 elections as opposed to the 1979 elections but the 1983 elections according to opponents of the N.P.N. was declared to be fraudulent and of mass rigging. This brings my attention to one of the favorite quotes of mine from Chief Obafemi Awolowo to me. In 1982, when Nigeria celebrated her first independence anniversary in Abuja the new capital and federal capital territory, President Shehu Shagari invited leaders of the opposition parties to celebrate the annual independence anniversary with him in order to asses progress being made in Abuja and to solicit advise from these leaders. At an airport departure ceremony I cornered Chief Obafemi Awolowo and asked him how does he feel about the ceremony and the progress being made in Abuja, he said to me "Tony, my brother and friend, you get to a stage in life you know so much you say so little". This also brings me back to Chief M.K.O. Abiola, during his famous escape from Nigeria due to threats on his life from the Babangida administration officials, we met in the United States and discussed at length. One of my memorable moments was when he finally left the U.S., to return to Nigeria en route London, I escorted him to the airport and personally was with him alone until he was seated at his seat in the first class cabin of a British airways aircraft, this was on September 3rd 1993 and the personal things we discussed , unfortunately I can not share with anyone, because as Chief Awolowo said " you get to a stage in life you know so much you say so little", but one of the things Chief Abiola told me that gave me hope for his safety was that on September 5th 1993, he called my house in Washington D.C. United States and informed me that he was going home to Nigeria and that his fellow Yoruba man who was the second-in-command in the Sanni Abacha regime (General Oladipo Diya) has assured him a safe return and that this is a new regime and that he should not be afraid because they (the Sanni Abacha administration) will look into the June 12 1993 Presidential election situation and either overturn the Babangida's annulment or recommend a new election. I was hopeful and happy because I know and thought I could trust General Oladipo Diya. In real life things seldom work out exactly as their designers intended, that is why I was astounded to hear that Chief Abiola declared himself President when a sitting military administration was still in power. One does not know why he did it, may be it was entrapment, because based on my discussions with Chief Abiola, I never expected him to do that, because, in order to declare himself President, he needs the backing of the entire military and it is the military that should have declared Chief Abiola as the President.

The economic and physical resources of a country, influence its foreign as well as its domestic policies. Because Nigeria's oil does not command much respect as it use to until the British emergence in the production of oil, that is why the United States is treating the Abiola and the Nigerian situation in a lukewarm manner.

I believe politics came about because people of differing and sometimes conflicting interests and beliefs sought to live and work together harmoniously. Every Nigerian government regardless of its political affiliation, be it military, must respond to the needs of the population.

Resources have been drained by military spending, knowing that we could not even fight a small country like Cameroun or carry out an effective peace keeping effort in Liberia, these resources could have been turned to economic growth in Nigeria.

Southern Nigerians have fared less well than the Northerners. The Southerners on a ratio have more education, worse jobs and lower incomes. Southerners lack the traditional rise from poverty to prosperity.

Citizens from the oil-producing states in Nigeria are the poorest of the poor. The biggest single industry in Nigeria is the military and is dominated by Northern Nigeria not by design but by foolishness on the part of Southern Nigeria.

N.T.A. REFLECTIONS

My good friend General Olusegun Obasanjo, while he was Head-Of-State of Nigeria, it was the Southern media and especially his own people the Yorubas who portrayed General Obasanjo as an illiterate, a sell-out and a no good Head-Of-State. But on several occasions, when I was Nigerian Television Authority (N.T.A.)news correspondent covering Presidential affairs (i.e. State House correspondent Ribadu Road Ikoyi) I had come across General Olusegun Obasanjo on numerous occasions including going to his farm in Otta to visit him personally, not only did I find General Obasanjo extremely intelligent but he was also a man who believe in planning (no wonder he liberated the oil-rich Rivers State during the civil war). Also on numerous occasions when General Obasanjo visited the United States between 1993 - 1994, we were often together and I can not once again share the numerous private discussions we had together, but one thing I can tell you is that General Obasanjo is neither an illiterate nor a sell-out. He has always believed in planning he says, in everything in life that succeeds, planning is the key difference, planning makes wishes come true. How I wish the Southern leaders would have capitalized on the fact that they have their own tribesman in power and work closely with him, may be 1979 elections would have been to the advantage of the Southerners.

One good advice for the government leadership, be it Southern or Northern, be it military or political party ---- the government should exist without the ability to tyrannize its citizens.

In Nigeria, a person need not be of any particular religion in order to hold public office, this is what is written in every constitution before and after amendments, why is the office of the Presidency any exception? The government of Nigeria and her people should resist by all means not to make one religion official religion of the country.

Equality and justice should be two of the basic values of all Nigerians and their government. Separation of power in every word means sharing of power. At all times, government and efficiency means that the government does not hire a farmer to be a health cabinet minister/secretary. The Southern elite has always claim that this is the practice of most administrations in Nigeria. One of the famous gossips is that the North always give the job of furniture maker to a seamstress.

I believe in the rule of the majority but also as long as the majority rules, the majority should also know that it's rule is not absolute. The minority can also influence the rulership of the majority. The Southerners feel that they have inadvertently become a permanent minority in Nigeria -- one that loses every election, a permanent minority that is never in a winning majority.

Most Southern Nigerians do not believe that they have a stake in the future of Nigeria, because they never get what they want out of the right to participate in government leadership. For so long, Southern Nigerians have been permanent minorities who are not even invited or admitted to the political process and eventually once invited and admitted, they saw themselves as permanent minorities who always lost. Those who see themselves as members of permanent minority that always loses may interpret their condition as a case of majority tyranny and may look to insurrection as the only way out. It is for these reasons that both the self-satisfied Northerner and the most militant Southerner are equally products of Nigerian political thought. The Northerner may praise Nigerian political process, while the Southerner may say these process always yield to Northern majorities that never allow Southern minorities to get what they want.

Learning something requires giving up time that could be spent doing other things, so also, anything successful takes planning and planning takes time, hence the South should take some time and plan very well for the future. Further Southern Nigeria advances in every sphere of life should come from individual efforts rather than only North/South militancy or government assistance.

The educated in any society are more influential, their political views have a greater chance of success than views of the uneducated, hence in this case, the South should have more influence in political leadership in Nigeria than the North because the South they say have more educated people than the North but unfortunately, the North is more cohesive and they are willing to work together.

The lines of division in the Southern political system are generally economics, regional, religious and ethnic background. While the North stick together regardless of economic, regional and ethnic background.

All human behavior is motivated by expectations of some kind of reward and the Northerners behavior is motivated by the fact that when they stick together their reward would be extremely big and when they fall apart like the Southerners, their reward would be infinetly small like the Southerners.

Human beings are not in politics for nothing. They want to get something out of it. They want to make a difference in their lives and their community and to a great extent in their country. Enthusiasm for causes is short-lived but the necessity of making a living, that is, earning a daily bread is permanent.

When you look at things, you find that political participation depends not only on individual's desire and ability to act but on whether that individual's action is cooperatively received by its targets.

Nothing is more dramatic than conflict and nothing about conflict seems simpler than labeling winners and losers. The future of any nation including Nigeria is more important than the past, Nigeria and Nigerians should use the present to plan and achieve better life for its citizens in the future.

When you look at the North/South political question, you find out that determination and physical stamina are among the most important qualification for a successful political career in Nigeria not necessarily academic qualifications.

In politics, generally among other things you have to be intelligent, ambitious, energetic, self-confident, strong-willed and politically experienced. Each politician is also affected (in his or her ways) by various political, economic and most of all social interests. That is why most times good politics is eighty (80) percent getting credit. This brings me to the situation of Nigerian Army corps of Engineers, the Nigerian Army Corps of Engineers should devote their time and energy to public works just like in the United States and other civilized countries, not ceremonious projects for the Army. When the Nigerian Army Corps of Engineers invest in public works, then they will get their eighty (80) percent of political credit for things being done to better the polity of the citizens of Nigeria.

Nigeria as I have asserted, should start planning for the future by looking at the present, but just because the future begins with the present is no reason for anyone to think that nothing ever changes. All things being equal, people should be prepared to change with the times. Because when you look at it, you can have an accurate picture of a problem but this does not guarantee a satisfactory solution, you still have to experiment until it works. That is why democracy is best thought of as a method of choosing leaders and this leaders have the human quality to be wrong at certain times but also to correct their wrongs when it is made known to them either through opposition or by experience. That is why equality and freedom are one of the two most important needs of a human being. Freedom to say or do whatever one pleases as long as it is in the realm of legality and equality of the human being, regardless of creed or state or origin.

Very high and continuous levels of instability will always affect most people adversely. Few human beings would like to live on day-to-day basis. Its very difficult to plan (you know planning is the difference in everything that succeeds not luck), if one does not know what laws and rulers will be in force from one month to the next or from one year to the next.

Why under any circumstances should a farmer plant more crops than his family or customer needs if any surplus will be stolen by marauders? It is also very hard to be a great painter if one's studio is shelled by the government today and bombed by rebels tomorrow. That is why governments anywhere in the world except Africa and Nigeria in particular strive for stability. Another reason is that, with the consequences of instability, yesterday's luxuries in every sector of Nigeria are now today's necessities.

Most government officials seek to use government as a

tool for improving the way they live instead of seeking government to improve the way the Nigerian populace live.

In every democracy, the leadership has the right to be wrong and correct its mistakes, but in Nigeria, each time the political leadership goes wrong, the military comes in through a coup purportedly to right the wrongs of politicians.

A sensible politician should rely more on experts when dealing about bridge building than when worrying about slums -- because construction engineers know how to build bridges, while sociologists have not yet demonstrated much skill in dealing with slums, so also, politicians have the expertise to deal with political leadership while the military has not demonstrated any skill in political affairs.

The military and the politicians however, have done a lot of good to the Nigerian polity but it is only news of failure that most people pay attention to than the successes of every administration. The reason is obvious, most people pay more attention to bad news because bad news and failure is more newsworthy.

Nigerians generally think that the government should be a constant source of help when the going is rough but not a constant presence in all aspects of their lives, rain or shine. One of the principal tasks of government is resolution, moderation and channeling of conflicts not permanent dictatorship.

Although, very often a solution may look good on paper, but its implementation may raise so many problems of conflict, power and the capacity that its implementation is not a good solution. But no matter how you look at it, politics should be the art of the possible.

Politics often consists of bringing many evaluations from many different viewpoints together and asking just how the grand plan will work out on a day-to-day basis for the people involved.

Nigerians should realize that nations are very different from one another. Each nation is so much a product of its own peculiar history and culture that we can never be certain if a procedure or policy which is successful in one country will work in another country, but Nigerians should at least try the good procedures or policies that have worked in other countries and improve on them.

Citizens satisfaction in political leadership, fosters political stability, willingness to obey the laws and most of all simple patriotism. But if the citizens are not satisfied with their political leadership, one of the key elements that gets eroded immediately is patriotism.

Citizens begin to see their government run by a few interest-groups instead of the interest group of the entire nation. Most times, the problem with the Nigerian government is the kind of people in office not the nature of the system -- be it military or politicians. People want good out of government even if it is a plutocracy, as long as those being governed feel that the system provides for them every of their needs.

Disagreement is inherent in human nature; it arises from individual differences in occupation, wealth, religion, ability, taste, temperament, race, opinion, and other human characteristics. Moreover, a certain level of dynamism, creativity and change is beneficial and when a society is changing, there is bound to be conflict. We may suspect that a society with a very low level of conflict is suffering from stagnation or oppression. The crucial point then, is the system's record in accommodating disagreements without stifling them. Does it facilitate the resolution of conflict? Does it impose a lockstep conformity or fan the flames of violence and hatred? These are the questions every responsible government or administration in Nigeria need to answer.

The world at large has seen many societies torn apart by relentless conflicts between factions that could not find peaceful means of resolving their differences and the world also have had too many political systems where every aspect of personal life is organized in government-controlled groups, where disputes are defined as sabotage or treason --- most times if you disagree or oppose any government in power in Nigeria, you are regarded as a saboteur or traitor and the secret police will make sure that you never resurface again.

Religion and politics continue to be a dangerous mixture anywhere in the world, hence the entire government of Nigeria at any given administration, should stay away from the bickering of religion. In Nigeria, it is precisely the fact that we have economic inequality and that we need political equality to protect the majority of the people who are poor from the abuse of the minority who are wealthy. Although, no country in the modern world have managed to achieve anything like equality no matter how much devotion to the principal they claim but at least they try.

In communist nations for example, income disparities are great among the different occupation and also among the same jobs in different regions. The former Soviet Union also provides special stores, housing, vacation facilities and medical care to political leaders and those in privileged occupations and positions. But one thing the United States of America does is to guarantee everyone (regardless of race or economic standing) the equal opportunity to be the best you can be in any of your legal endeavors.

Every category of a society's existence is a valid measure of its government performance. What Nigeria and her governments need are those who care; one person can make a great difference in any little way he or she can. Knowledge is power and money is power, Nigeria has both knowledge and money, the only way to control both is to harness the two without wasting any of the two. Knowledge in every sense is the understanding gained by experience. All Nigerians should understand that helping others to help themselves is the best assistance everyone can offer.

One of the major problems in sustaining a political administration in Nigeria is that its leaders were reluctant political players who never did aspire to be President but were compromised for others who aspire to be President, hence the lop-sided way they led the country without strength or direction. A leader who aspired to be an elected President, definitely will have strength, vision and a determination to choose service Chiefs whom he knows believe in the Political process of leadership and these service Chiefs will in turn educate their men and women to follow orders from their civilian bosses and not harbor an ulterior motive of plotting a coup.

I believe that you can have anything in the world that you want, simply by helping enough other people to get what they want. This is one thing that the Northern part of Nigeria do so well and that is the key to empowerment not selfish deeds but upliftment of your fellow human being regardless of where they are from.

My first encounter on the threshold between North and South, started at Nigeria Television Authority (N.T.A.). Myself and hundreds of other Nigerians both male and female applied to N.T.A. network news, we were short-listed based on qualifications and invited to an audition, after the audition we were short-listed again based on telegenic appearance and diction, then we were invited for interview. On the day of the interview (early 1981), when it was my turn to be interviewed, I was ushered in by a female assistant, to the board-room of the Managing Director of N.T.A. Network news and I was made to introduce myself while all the interview board-members introduce themselves to me. The chairman of the interview-board was Alhaji Mohammed Ibrahim and he was also the Managing Director of N.T.A. Network news. After series of question and answers, Alhaji Mohammed Ibrahim then asked the other interview-board members if they have any more questions, if not he thinks he is through with this applicant, ---- immediately he said that, one of the interviewers got up and took my diploma and went close to a fluorescent light and stretched his arm with the diploma in his hand towards the light and said "you know this America graduates they can do fraudulent things, let us make sure that this is not a fraudulent diploma before We employ this man", Alhaji Mohammed Ibrahim then snapped in an irate voice, "I do not think that, that is a necessary comment, this man is obviously very talented, personable and very telegenic, I think this man will be an asset to the network news department, if there is no other question, that is the end of this interview, thank you Mr. Tony Oyatedor, you will hear from us soonest".

Two weeks after my interview with N.T.A. network news, I received a letter of employment and started working at N.T.A., but I found out that the man who was objecting to my employment was a Southerner and until I left N.T.A. he made sure my stay in N.T.A. was a living hell. To start with, myself and a young man Mr. Come Oviaghele were employed to anchor the 7 p.m. news as a way of getting used to the way Nigeria news organizations operate, because we were both

U.S.A. trained broadcasters, but to our greatest astonishment, Mr. Oviaghele and myself only anchored the 7 p.m. news once and we were both removed immediately by this same Southerner and relegated to reportorial assignments, but all through this time, Alhaji Mohammed Ibrahim had gone to Mecca for hajj and on his return he went on vacation, but when he returned from vacation he was astounded to see that we were not anchoring the news, this Southerner had told him all sorts of stories, but Alhaji Mohammed Ibrahim non the less encouraged Mr. Oviaghele and myself to stay calm, that he will ensure that we go back to anchoring the news and report the news at the same time, which he did. With these and so many other incidences later, I started learning that the Southerner will rather bury you than uplift you, (not all of them but most Southerners).

Southerners, we must start investing on people instead of investing on houses, cars and business. Alhaji Bilyaminu Usman, one time federal minister of education, once said to me "if you have a friend or brother who is vying for the position of the Presidency, would you help this person or would you bring him down? --- If you help this person it means you can always tell people that -- my brother or my friend is the President but if you bring this person down, can you say your person is in the Presidency"? There lies the difference between the South and the North. The North invests on people but the South invests on property. Next time when you see Shehu goes, Mohammadu come, Mohammadu goes, incomes Ibrahim and when Ibrahim goes, incomes Sanni, do not feel bad because while you were investing on properties they were investing on people.

A northerner would rather help his friend or brother to succeed but a Southerner would rather bring the brother or friend down. At one time in N.T.A. network news, the position of Director of news was vacant under the Director

37

Generalship of Dr. Walter Ofonagoro, we had three eligible people on the same grade level to ascend the position, all three people were Southerners all three were very good friends (so they thought), each of these candidates went separately to Dr. Ofonagoro and bad mouth the other two, Dr. Ofonagoro found out that he can not appoint neither of these three people without offending the other two, hence he went to Bauchi State and brought a northerner from N.T.A. Bauchi and made him Director of News (D.N.) And all these three Southerners became loyal to this Northerner. Imagine if one of them was the D.N. in a unique setting, wont the other two benefit from him based on good friendship? Would you also blame this on Northerners, I do not think so.

When you see a new high-rise office building under construction -- notice that when construction begins it seems like it takes months and months almost forever before you see it begin to rise out of the ground. But once it gets above ground-level it seems to rise about one floor per week --- it goes up fast. That is the situation of the Northern part of Nigeria, they started slowly empowering their people, to them at the beginning it looked like it will take forever but now they are almost everywhere on a weekly basis and the Southerners are now agitated. But look at the hands that rock the cradle, it is the Southerners who brought these on themselves by not planning for the future and seeing only now and doing selfish things.

SOUTHERNERS AND RESPONSIBILITY

It is about time that the people of Southern Nigeria claim responsibility for their actions. For some time now, all you hear about is how the Northern elite of the Hausa/Fulani tribe has been ruling Nigeria, but people forget that Nigeria did have Southern Nigerians of the likes of General Ironsi, Statesman Zik and General Obasanjo as leaders or President or Head-Of-State of Nigeria.

The blame that Southerners stick on Northerners and the cries that Nigeria is not one and should not be one is like South Africa or Zimbabwe citizens calling for separation of a white state and black state due to earlier oppression by whites on blacks.

The same principle carried out by President Mandela and President Mugabe were the ideals dished out by General Yakubu Gowon (after the civil war in Nigeria), the three R's -- reconstruction, rehabilitation and reconciliation.

Unless you have not seen war/revolution and peace, but if you have seen any of these, you will know and be gratified that peace is better and you will appreciate peace. Look at the Haiti situation -- peace prevailed over aggression. The overwhelming call for civil war or revolution and insinuations that Nigeria should be divided into its three major ethnic group is absurd. Due to self destruction and marginalization, people forget that Nigeria has four major ethnic groups --- Hausa, Igbo, Yoruba and Ijaw. Even at that, who says the Uroboh's, the Nupe's, the Ishan's etc. do not want their own country?

The United Sates of America is the only country in the

world where you have all race, color, ethnic, religion and different backgrounds of origin gathered together in one nation and they are prospering despite the racial divide. The United States of America is blessed for having Olajuwon, the Fords, Rockefella's Perot , Colin Powell, Jesse Jackson, General John Shalikashvili, Judge Lance Ito, Donna Shalala just to name a few.

Nigerians should be proud of prosperity in diversity. Sure, I know of the fact that there is no freedom to do what you want and power and wealth is being shared by a few people. Southerners once had power but due to envy and greed they never put transfer of power into the hands of their brothers and sisters. The me alone generation, me and my family alone should be superstar while my fellow brothers and sisters should continue to beg for alms from me generation are the roots of the Southern tragedy.

Decades ago, the Southerners had people at the helms of affairs in the military but these people never thought about the future, they only think about the present hence they never made transition of power to their fellow Southerners. There was a time when Southerners had people like D. Ejoor (Army), N.B. Soroh (Navy), E. Kentebe (Navy), S. Adewusi (Police), Akinwale Wey (Navy), A. Akirinrinade (Army), just to name a few, but now you have a situation where the northerners are bent on transition of power between themselves, that is, they invest on people not property, that is why you have the transition of power from Shehu Shagari to Muhammadu Buhari, from Buhari to Ibrahim Badamasi Babangida, from Babangida to Sanni Abacha.

The clear fact remains, the problem is between the Southerners, you Southerners must wake up and clean your house, revolution of the mind is the only thing that will help, Southerners must stop blaming the Northerners but

40

themselves and their previous generation, now is the time for change, like the late founder of North Korea told his people: "WE ENVY NO ONE", so also should the Southern Nigerian start on that path, envy no one, help your fellow brothers and sisters to get up, then the burden would be less on you and there would be more prosperity in your community and the country. Do not try to be the only superstar in your family, help others while you help yourself . Do not look at your fellow Southerner who is successful with envy and try to put him or her into trouble, instead be happy for him or her and pray to God for your own success and work towards it. It is time to stop blaming others and start the wave of change for a better future by helping others to stand. Change is difficult but change is good. A wise man changes for the better but a fool remains the same. So, Southerners, are you going to be wise and change now or be a fool and remain the same, the choice is yours.

The game of putting North and South against each other is a distraction, let Southerners stop killing each other, stop burning the houses of your fellow Southerners, stop the greed that makes you steal from each other, stop the indolence that prevents us from teaching our children ethics, good morals and spirit of oneness in Nigeria. Above everything else, do not blame others for the situation in the South, get up wake up and make a change for a better and prosperous Nigeria, ONE NIGERIA WITH UNITY AND PRIDE FOR COMMUNITY SERVICE.

Nigeria has to be a country where all of her citizens can aspire to be President regardless of what part of Nigeria they are from. Nigeria is a country of approximately 120 million people yet the country dances with just about 120 people for the past 35 years. In every administration, you see the any-government-in-power (AGIP) syndrome people ---- Ojukwu, Jakande, Ogbemudia, Babatope, Nwobodo, Maitama Sule,

Shehu Musa etc. It is very foolish of the country to keep going back to these same people, these same failed leadership, administration after administration.

General Abacha, during his first prominence in the Nigerian polity , announced , in 1983, in his coup broadcast that toppled the Shagari administration, he called the civilian administration corrupt and inept, yet he found it necessary in 1993 to bring some of the then civilian governors in 1983 to his cabinet --- Jim Nwobodo, Abubakar Rimi, Lateef Jakande just to name a few. Why is it that General Sanni Abacha could not try other Nigerians, Nigerians with vision and self-less service are rotting away in Nigeria, in the U.S.A., in Europe and other parts of the world, while these few (120 Nigerians) continue to be on-again members of every administration. Decades of so-called independence yet no progress, we keep retrogressing instead of progressing, it is about time we put some young blood, new faces and new ideas with new vision in to the Nigerian polity.

A nation's internal resiliency based on food is more important to her survival than anything . Although, agriculture is not all that the Northern part of Nigeria has, there has been numerous reports that gold and oil of commercial quantity have been unearthing at various parts of the North.

Southerners in the oil-producing states in the east, claim that the Northerners with the help of the Yorubas in the South have taken money emanating from oil sales to build schools, highways, huge buildings and hospitals in the North and parts of the west while the eastern states that produce the oil are rotting.

The North is enjoying all the resources created by the South yet they are somehow not together as one might perceive but in general terms they are more together than the whole South.

The Northern numerical power etymologized from joining all the provinces above the Niger-Benue river into one Northern region is the focus of the North being called the North up till this moment despite the multiplication of states starting from the creation of twelve states by General Yakubu Gowon administration. Right now, many ethnic and religious minority groups from the North have since emancipated themselves. The so-called middle-belt states of Kogi, Plateau, Taraba, Benue, Kwara and Adamawa states are all fighting for separate identity from the entrenched North. But the one North is still entrapped amongst them. Amongst other reason, for self-identification purposes by these so-called middle-belt states, the late Major Orka, announced during his abortive coup attempt of 22nd of April 1990, that the other states in the North, especially Sokoto State, should be conditionally excised from the Federal Republic of Nigeria.

The forces in the middle-belt states and the internal political differences in the North might arouse a bigger problem than one expects. Most of the conflicts arise from the oppressiveness of the Northern elite. Majority of the ordinary people in the North are virtually sentenced to a life of political irrelevance, poverty and illiteracy. The poor are told by the elite to endure a permanent life of hardship while the elite is blessed to enjoy followership and loyalty of the poor and the downtrodden.

The Northern conservatives are in alliance with the progressives in the North in ascertaining that the constant domination of Nigerian politics by the conservative elite in the North had sparked so many mishaps to the entire North.

The North might split politically on ideological lines, the privileged conservative ruling class might face the risk of collapsing under the determined attack of the progressives in the North. The tradition of echoing a unified North is already on the verge of collapsing.

The Ijaws and Southern Nigerians are sitting down like they are watching a soccer game. They are watching the Northerners decide the future of Nigeria all alone. But I do not in all fairness lay the blame on the Northerners, it is partially the fault of the Southerners.

The Southerners have been very lazy, very passive in demanding their legal rights. Southern Nigerians of the early sixties were afire with the spirit of nationalism. But now, the generation born after the oil boom are so lazy and complacent. Nigeria has become a country that obsesses over military coups while ignoring an increasingly angry poor underclass. A country where most of the wealth and power is controlled by the top one (1) percent of the population while the bottom ninety-nine (99) percent scrape to get by. The civil rights movements in the Unites States Of America was born in the churches in the Southern parts of the U.S. where segregations was knee deep in the country. What rights will the churches in the Southern part of Nigeria fight for?

My definition of having it made is -- having more money than you can spend and the time to spend it. Also, in my opinion, it is a fact that you will never have it made working for someone else. Most Southern Nigerians are working in all sorts of jobs in the U.S.A. with very few investing and having their own business, and when they do have their own business, their fellow Nigerians would not patronize them. Only heaven knows the enormous proportion of money (hard currency in dollar) that Nigerians waste on frivolities in the

U.S.A. A typical Southern Nigerian would drive a cab for a living, reside in a one-bedroom apartment and drive a Mercedes Benz as his private car, he would organize a birthday party and spend hundreds (sometimes thousands) of dollars in all sorts of wasteful ventures.

Spanish people who know where they came from and know where they are going, crowd themselves in one-room apartments and save their money (hard-earned dollars) and send it to their underprivileged parents, brothers and sisters for their up-keep.

Southern Nigerians who live in Nigeria in poverty situations, the moment they arrive in the U.S.A., they forget where and what situation they came from and they forget where they are going. Most younger Southern Nigerians, when they arrive and are jobless within the first few days of their arrival, they will call their older brother, --- uncle or bros, after they get a job, they will start calling their older brothers by their first name. I had a situation where a younger relative of mine who use to call me uncle Tony in Nigeria, when he arrived in the U.S.A., he started calling me bros Tony, when he started working and lived in his own apartment, my name became simply Tony, when I became irate because he was calling me by first name basis, he told me that we are in America, that America is a leveler.

The disunity amongst Southern Nigeria anywhere (especially in the U.S.A.) is so prevalent and ludicrous that you only need to look into your immediate family to see and know what I am talking about.

Lack of respect for Nigerians abroad especially in the U.S.A., is one of major concern. The Southern Nigerian in the United States Of America most of the time, is the one driving taxi for a living, washing dishes, etc., and also it is the

Southern Nigerian that does fraudulent things like credit card fraud and the most degrading of all -- drug trafficking.

In the early 1960's, if you told anybody in the U.S. that you are from Nigeria they look at you with awe, but not any more, Nigerians are now looked at as thieves, drug pushers, con-men/women, everything bad is associated with Nigerians. I am yet to see any Northern Nigerian in jail for any drug offense or fraudulent offense in the United States.

The Southern Nigerian family in the U.S., despise one another instead of loving one another. When they are in Nigeria they may appear to love one another but the moment they arrive in the U.S. and start to earn money for a living they start to show their true color of envy for one another.

A family is supposed to be a unit brought together by common bond of blood, genetics, commonality of history, culture and of language in a common place. The outward pressure of earning money to survive in the U.S., and greed is tearing the Southern Nigerian families apart. Unity and real love between Southern Nigeria and Northern Nigeria can not surface or take shape until Southern Nigerians unite amongst themselves and the first place for Southern Nigerians to start is to unite amongst their own families.

Lack of knowledge is the number one destroyer of the Southern Nigeria family. Ignorance is the one enemy of the Southern Nigerian family. Ignorance and the knowledge of self pride in family unity should be looked into.

Southern Nigerians must understand that today is built on the activities of yesterday and if you do not know what happened yesterday that brought you to where you are today, then you might as well forget about what is going to happen tomorrow. The only way to solve yesterday and today's problem so that it does not occur tomorrow is by intelligent dialogue not by violent acts against each other. Southern Nigerians must lift each other's hearts, spirits and hopes. Because when Northerners have differences, it is based on principles not pettiness, intrigue and envy.

Nigerian government should really do something to counteract what Nigerians in the U.S. sees as the media's practice of treating Nigerians and crime as synonymous. It is very few Nigerians who are involved with crime who are making it look bad for every Nigerian due to biased media coverage in the United Sates Of America.

Southerners unquestionably, spent an overwhelming enormous proportion of time fighting amongst themselves rather than loving themselves. They are also too in-ward looking instead of out-ward looking. Southern Nigerians for the first time since independence have no clear leader. They have virtually become a body without a head and it is attributed to jealousy, intrigue and self-interest.

Recently, most Southerners have been debating either to assimilate (as it is now) with Northerners or separate (for the future). People forget that the North and South have inter-married and that they have produced children from these marriages and these kids whom neither belong to the North nor South have also grown and married and produce children of their own. Where will all these children belong? The people agitating for separation should answer that question.

The Southern leadership is suffering from built-in stagnation which comes when leadership is allowed to perpetuate itself. We hear of the same names in the political leadership of the South since independence, while the names in the North keeps changing hence, these give the impression that the North is dominating the South. The South has to be more inclusionary in regards to appointments not naming the same people to different positions at all times. Southerners should try to be equitable in regards to utilization of skills and try not to do anything that would antagonize people in the process of trying to nominate people into positions of power.

Southerners must stop having animosity and ill will against each other. As much as the South needs different leadership, the Southern leadership should not spend more time being different and effective. Instead of having internal conflicts in the South, leaders should bring themselves together and discuss all possible means of empowerment in Southern Nigeria.

Southerners should realize that the simple but most important gifts that money can not buy are -- kindness, thoughtfulness, courtesy, consideration and good nature.

A warm friendly smile to one another is appropriate to any situation. Every Southerner should be generous towards his fellow Nigerian regardless of the region he or she is from, by being generous, I really do not mean generous with money only, I mean generous in his or her judgements. Tolerance is the key word, wait before you judge, until you know why this person acts or lives as he or she does.

Not a single Nigerian (North or South) could live within themselves; Nigerians must, if they are to be truly happy, have a sense that, they like each other and value what they can do for each other and appreciate what they have in single undivided country. Do not envy one another, praise one another instead. He or she who praises another person enriches himself or herself far more than he or she does the one praised, to praise is an investment in happiness. The poorest human being also has something to give that the rich could not buy hence every human being rich or poor must appreciate one another.

Nigerians should also know that the future depends on the concrete plans and investments they make. Nigerians should put their money where their future is, Nigeria and Nigerians have to dare to be great. Fear is the key that unlocks the doors of opportunity. You get what you pay for --- that is, you either invest big now for the future or play around and let the future catchup with you.

GOVERNMENT ACTIVITY

Nigeria has lost her regional/international respect due to her leaders squandering of her wealth and this ultimately has shown Nigeria and her leaders that regional/international cooperation requires mutual respect. Freedom in any part of the world is meaningless without the security the community and the state can provide. Nigerians and (Africans as a whole) need to get more of her people to care for each other.

What happens to Nigeria in the coming decade is largely up to Nigerians not foreign countries. Everyone in Nigeria is for change in general but they are afraid for change in particular. Nigerian leaders need to invest in the future of Nigerians to remain free.

Nigerian government should stop serving itself and the economic elite, the government (any government -- military or civilian) should start serving the Nigerian people and putting the Nigerian people first not last. The government (be it military or civilian) should stop rewarding themselves and concentrate on the well- being of the people by making them to be more productive and invest on future growth of the Nigerian economy for the benefit of the people of Nigeria. The ultimate agenda is to shift from the present to the future and do so with precision. The rich, the elite and the educated should not withdraw themselves into another kind of suburban slum -- big residential houses with iron gates and brick walls and then refuse to assist their fellow citizen. Money comes and goes so does fame but it is the people that you assist that will always be with you when you are down.

In a difficult time, people do not want someone to beat them up, they need someone to help them up. It is time for the elite, the well-educated, and the rich to catch the downtrodden and help them up.

Nigeria is the only country I know where the government will not encourage farmers to farm in excess before banning some type of agriculture, we do not have enough wheat yet the government found it necessary to ban U.S. wheat from the country, we did not have enough home-grown rice yet we ban rice from the outside world; any country that want to restructure any part of the economy needs to do so gradually and do it right. In Nigeria, they want to restructure certain parts of the economy overnight without a gradual process of planning and ensuring that the country has enough of whatever they want to plan.

Nigerian government wants rapid reform and they forget that rapid reform includes extreme readjustment and excruciating excessive pain, but gradual reform with effective planning will eliminate pain outright.

Nigerian government must put her people first and give them jobs which will ultimately make them responsible citizens. Nigerian people must be hopeful and not have a sense of hopelessness, Nigerian people need a sense of possibility and the only way to achieve this is by good and self-less leadership. The leadership must empower the citizens. The federal government of Nigeria must invest in the future of the people. Nigerians regardless of their current position must take personal responsibility for the future of Nigeria as a country.

People must sacrifice today so as to get a better tomorrow but the sacrifice should be across the board and it should be gradual.

Coups and counter-coups are apparently not the answer to good government . If you have any constructive view, channel it to the appropriate quarters and stop destructive ideas. Nigeria must go forward period.

The President or Head-of-Sate does not govern alone, the people have to be willing to be governed and the cabinet members have to carry out the administration's policy in a clear, concise and effective manner. The Nigerian public have to understand the policies of the government and abide by it but the leadership must draft the framework for people to understand.

Nigerian people are unwilling to sacrifice or wait any longer for the Nigerian economy to bounce back. The Nigerian government can not cut people off from the changes their government is making. The Nigerian government can not continue to neglect the poor masses and also continue the kinds of financial mismanagement that led to currency crisis in the country.

With the economic crisis in the country and pledge of national sacrifice, the unity of the country should be paramount in the hearts of the citizens. The leadership's agenda at all times should not conflict with the will of the people.

As long as the Nigerian economy is open to the world for investments, inflation would be controlled by market forces, the economic growth would be healthy and productivity will rise.

Obviously , Nigeria is still a developing country, no one can change that by decree. Obviously, previous leadership of the Nigerian economy have made some major mistakes, no one can pin-point any simple factor as the cause of today's economic crisis but what I can attribute it to, is a combination of political blunders, economic miscalculations, squandering of oil wealth and just plain bad luck.

Clear signs of political instability has thus far prompted financial markets to react with panic. The government should not keep growth down to dampen inflation but at the same time the government should be enormously pressured to share the wealth of the people with the people.

Most of the leadership do not go hog-wild when they change economic policy and the leadership also always guess wrong in the way they handle economic policy changes, now unfortunately, it is the Nigerian people who are taking the hard-hit of economic log-jam.

The notion of silencing political opposition instead of listening to them should come to a screeching halt. Nigerian problem is rooted in lack of discipline and lack of priorities. The leadership should get the economy growing. Any leader any where in the world can not lead without listening. The Nigerian leadership must listen to the yearnings of the people.

The present generation of leadership must focus their attention on two priorities --- 1. educational reform and 2. economic development.

The only way the leadership can regain the people's unavoided attention and ultimately their trust is with genuine and effective leadership. People want government that works for the benefit of the people not for the sole benefit of administration officials. People want a government that creates economic growth, reduces crime, improves school (especially in the rural areas) and help the people to find opportunities they need to succeed. People want a more efficient government and they are looking for a more effective government. Government must help people to equip themselves to solve their problems. Government must be a positive force in the lives of the people. People want a government that offers them opportunities they need to improve their lives, people want the government to expand opportunities for Nigerians by reinventing and rethinking its role in job security, education, health care and affordable housing for every citizen regardless of his or her region or religion. Government should work for the people not against the people.

The poor masses of Nigeria know in their heart, that the elite has no idea what it is like to raise children in an economy where there is no hope, disintegration of values turn upside down, an economy where violence and visions of instant gratification co-exist with crime.

As Head-Of-State or President,, the leadership is the leader of the people first and leader of the government second. The most important role for any leader is to communicate a vision so compelling that it must affect the decisions of people in their private lives and in the public institutions.

The developed world is in a transition between the industrial era to the age of information super-highway but Nigeria has not yet arrived at the industrial era. Nigeria should change and rethink the way government must act on the value of education, about government relationship with the poor masses.

The leadership should challenge every Nigerian to commit themselves to new kinds of learning, new kinds of cooperation, new kinds of responsibility as parents, students and members of the community.

There should be a new economic order in which the government acts like a partner with the private sector in improving schools in other to create a lifetime learning process for every Nigerian. Government should be willing to create opportunities for the people but the people themselves and their communities must also take responsibility for their growth and actions.

Government can not and should not do everything for the country, wealthy private citizens are the ones to put millions of Naira into urban development. Philanthropic deeds are not just throwing/spraying money at night parties or giving out scholarship money. Wealthy benefactors or captains of industry should work with the government in developing rural and urban areas.

Nigeria needs an economic lift from her wealthy citizens both at home and broad through community service so as to achieve total economic empowerment of her citizens. Nigeria needs more privately funded projects. People must stop viewing every project as the responsibility of the federal government. Community based projects by individuals will be among the miracles that will reverse Nigeria's sagging economic fortunes.

Everyone (both citizens and private or public corporations) must think of the country as their own responsibility not just the federal government's responsibility.

Nigeria has the vast family fortunes and generational wealth prevalent in most advance countries but the country is not blessed with the civil-minded largess of wealthy and prominent families. Business titans must be expected to use their corporate tills to build large projects for the sake of civil duty and on the premise that business and the country has a stake in the success of the community, in a sense, to invest in the community is to invest in the company itself. There is a parallel interest between business and community because they have the same goal ---empowerment. What is good for the community is also good for the business. If wealthy Nigerians do their part, it could and would go a long way toward altering the philanthropic mind-set that keeps people looking to the federal government for answers to everything.

Politics at all times is supposed to be strategic but in reality, politics at all times is always tactical. Nigeria needs a new generation of leadership because the current leadership is out of touch with the people of Nigeria. Being a leader is not just reading speeches but being there for the masses of Nigeria when and where they need you and to serve by good example.

Southern Nigeria with her minority mentality claim, must and should stop being an obstructionist. The new generation of leaders should always stay on the offensive line and must not allow the old brigade to set the agenda of running the country. The country needs intellectuals with good political skills, someone that would not be satisfied to be a theorist but someone that would be eager to run his ideas into action. Some one that will come into government with the sole purpose of changing Nigeria's economic slide from economic downturn to economic fortunes. This person must have a combination of sound economic judgement and common sense.

Most Nigerian public servants need to know the clear distinction between private disagreement and public loyalty to the leadership, this is necessary in order to promote a coherent message with one voice at all times -- because one of the first rules that a politician should realize is that perception equals reality.

The cornerstone for improving the economic lot of the Nigerian people is self-empowerment. The military in

Nigeria had maintained power for so long that the ambitious, talented and the intellectuals in Nigeria have either left the country or are in jail. The sure path to leadership or wealth in the country is unfortunately not through politics but through the military. This trend has made the military inflict violence against the country's elite. Instead of the military to serve the people they are suppose to defend in the advent of war, the military gives the people constant pain. This process must change. The military must stop the imprisonment of its citizens due to flimsy excuses.

While the rest of the world is growing richer, the Nigerian people are getting more miserable and poor. The military either stop in-humanity to their fellow men and women or the people they have held captive for long would in time work through their fears and rivalries and fight for their freedom.

It is time for Nigeria's leadership to rise above partisan politics and self-interest but above all, the leadership should get the job done. It is very impractical to pursue policies in the national interest that completely eliminate risk of suffering to some sectors alone. Governing by emotion is short-sighted and in the long run potentially very disastrous.

I am a big advocate of individual empowerment, I believe in helping individuals generate wealth for themselves instead of addicting people to constant government aid. People should know they are going to find their way to economic freedom only by depending on themselves and on their own discipline and creativity.

The fabrics that make a society civilized are -- integrity, industry, duty and responsibility. Self-help and Self-respect are the keys to empowerment.

The entire nation of Nigeria must realize that it is about

time we put our children and the future of the country first, the Nigerian nation depends on it. People should enter politics so as to make a difference.

The Nigerian leadership needs three priorities: - 1. raising Nigerians standard of living, 2. streamlining government and 3. strengthening the military -- to strengthen the military by improving war readiness, to ensure that the Armed forces can purchase new weapons systems and modernize their operations but not to strengthen the military for the use of civilian abuse.

The privilege new generation of Nigeria are the sons and daughters of the nations top officials (especially the military) who have had the kind of up-bringing that the poor masses could only imagine -- mansions, servants, cars, special schools and periodic travels abroad. These new privileged generation have not been schooled by their parents about the uncertainty of politics and the uncertainty of life itself. The Nigerian leadership can not ask its people to be better citizens, if its leadership can not be better servants.

Nigerians all over the world should also note that whatever every Nigerian does (instead of blaming the government at all times) the first question he or she should ask him or herself is -- is it good for Nigeria?

We as Nigerians have to change the focus of the Nigerian political system from personal character assassinations to reasoned and responsible debates about the issues that affects the country.

We have to make government to change the future and change what is possible. No government should engage in profiting from human misery. Most government in Nigeria have been sucking out money from the people who own the oil. People in oil-rich states would rather not have a bridge or electricity than see their oil rich citizens suffer. Government should be more than a business, government should be compassionate.

If the Northerners see themselves as revolutionaries, the Southerner should stop seeing themselves as reactionaries. Nigerians regardless of what part or what ethnic group you belong to must have to fix the boat together without sinking it, you can not burn Nigeria in order to built it, Nigeria must and should be built by builders, thinkers and self-less service not by detractors, destructionists and self-first.

The Nigerian people must ensure that laws are supreme and serve as a check on the nation's leadership rather than as tools the rulers can manipulate. Presently, the Nigerian leadership rules by proclamation and serves in legal cases as prosecutors, judge and jury. Nigeria's future depends on the establishment of rule of law, an improved legal system using the law as the ultimate authority and safeguarding of democracy and fundamental human rights.

Nigerians must attach great importance to building a strong legal system and strive to attain the point where laws will be followed, laws will be strictly and fairly enforced and lawless conduct will be prosecuted.

The concept of the rule of law has been a flimsy one in Nigeria. For a long while, the law has either been ignored or treated as a malleable implement in the hands of the leaders for keeping the population under control. Nigerian leaders want rule by law, not rule of law. The difference, is that under the rule of law, the law is preeminent and can serve as a check against the abuse of the power but under the rule by law, the law can serve as a mere tool for a government that suppresses people in a legalist fashion. There are good laws and there are bad laws but unlike the United States of America, Nigeria has no provision by which laws can be declared unconstitutional.

The Nigerian people want better economic lives and as they get more money they want to protect what they have worked hard to earn, they do not want a situation where someone can take these things from them by force. Many of today's leaders and senior civil servants suffer arbitrary arrest, humiliation or banishment. The rule of law should become an accepted and respected way of governing in Nigeria. Many leading democracy or human rights activist laws do not seem to apply. In several instances, the government has found legalistic ways of accomplishing the same thing it usually does by simply declaring someone as a coup plotter. Several outspoken critics of the government in power have been jailed on trumped-up charges. In a place like Nigeria, with a despotic tradition, an elaborate legal code serves as a more sophisticated instrument of rule by the government.

The criminal legal system in Nigeria is still a one-edged sword that only cuts downward especially with the Southerners. If a Southerner and a Northerner both commit a similar crime, chances are that the Southerner will go to jail but the Northerner will be acquitted.

Nigerian government has made some progress in passing laws (or decrees) but the biggest problem is enforcement. The legal system is in such quandry that corrupt judges are another problem. Lawyers are often pressured to make payments or seek favor with judges.

The leadership always wants to appear sensitive to the widespread discontent about public corruption both in high and low quarters. The poor masses always complain about

61

the people in power, the Nigerian people say they do not know the goals of their leaders, the general population live in total darkness of their leaders ideology and the future plans of economic stability of a nation that is one of the largest oil producers in the world. Years of economic and political mismanagement and total greed have brought about this situation of hopelessness. Since the leaders did not plan for the future, the populace has also joined the bandwagon where people only see today and forget about tomorrow, everybody (including leadership) wants to grab whatever he or she can grab today and the future is left in limbo. All these money hungry attitude and greed at all levels is having a very deep pathos effect on the younger generations whose future unquestionably remains hostage to yet undetermined outcome. People live with fear in their stomachs and heart twenty four (24) hours a day. There are daily stories of brothers killing brothers and sons killing their fathers and vice versa.

The Nigerian leadership has always been and continues to be a system based on greed, money, passion, (not compassion) and power. It has always survived because of mutual protection by everyone involved, you scratch my back I will scratch your back syndrome.

Nigeria is currently under financial instability and sinking living standards. Nigerian leadership either continues on the path of political and economic change or drifts back to the kinds of corrupt practices that for decades have enriched a small elite class. If the system is going to change in Nigeria, it has to start from the top not just the political leadership but the entire educated elite. Nigerians all over the world should live to make life better for other people.

With the present generation of Nigerians, there tends to be more despair not much hope. The federal government should be compassionate enough to help the poor and the helpless.

The agenda of the political leadership in Nigeria should be the eradication of poverty, unemployment and social disintegration. People in Nigeria are so impoverished (amidst plenty) that half of them go hungry every day.

NIGERIAN LEADERSHIP

The Nigerian leadership should set an action program to vanquish poverty and injustice. Improved development in Nigeria could only occur after corruption is banished from top to bottom and basic human rights are guaranteed for every Nigerian citizen.

The future strength of Nigeria is not a powerful military, is not big budget allocation for the defense department, the future strength is in the people of Nigeria. The Nigerian leadership should invest on the people of Nigeria. The country needs good health care and caring attitude from the elite.

Nigerian leaders have spent too much time and money on the present and the past and very little attention and money have been spent on the future. Money should be spent on the future for investments on research and development, infrastructure, environment , health care and most of all education. All these require able leadership, organization and the will to govern without fear or favor.

Nigerian leaders should put human rights above property rights, they should also stop being arrogant and inaccessible. Their code of conduct should be loyalty, decency and honor.

Every leader must put in place a reminder that because he or she suffered, there will be more joy. There are many rural and inner-city areas in Nigeria that are medically under served or not served at all. A healthy Nigeria is a better Nigeria, a healthy child is a better learner. The ultimate price of illiteracy translates into poverty and humiliation. The Nigerian child needs food, shelter and above all a caring federal government with stability. A more literate Nigeria would benefit the country and rid her from crime, unemployment, pollution, teenage pregnancy and poverty.

Feeding the hungry and housing the poor should be a priority to the federal leadership. Nigerian leaders have to ensure that before they criticize the President or Head-Of-State, they must have solutions. The leader should also work for the good of others. The definition of a successful life must include service to others.

The greatest assets of any country are its people. You must ensure that they are educated. Political stability is essential and the only way to make people have strong confidence in Nigeria is constitutional democracy.

You can not have security in any nation without economic and social development. Most Nigerians complain that the foreign media always show the slums part of ghetto areas of Lagos and other big cities of Nigeria but how many of these same Nigerians have suggested to the government about maintenance and general daily cleaning of all facilities and infrastructures.

Science and engineering must be promoted in Nigeria as exciting, sports can not and will not lead Nigeria into the 21st century. Science and engineering will lead Nigeria forever.

I think and I know that it is very good to have a strong sense of religion and a belief in God, I do not think going to church or mosque is the only way to religion, it takes being a good person and being a generous human being to everybody. Life is not getting and having but being and becoming. Who we are and what we will be tomorrow is how our fellow creatures will remember us.

It takes a great heart and courage to beat poverty and lots of passion to become successful. Every Nigerian has to make tomorrow better in light of yesterday. Like everything in life, you get what you pay for, you get what you invest. Nothing mandates you to stay where you are. Nigeria can only get out of the present doldrums by a massive investment in the future and the people of Nigeria. You can not plant corn and harvest beans hence Nigerians must build their community and plan for the future.

If the previous and past leaders had thought of Nigeria first and not their selfish interest, they would have planned for the future of Nigeria and Nigeria would not be in the economic dilemma that the country is in today.

Spending on clothing, fancy cars and extravagant night parties is a lot easier when a nation is not planning for the future, which is what Nigeria and Nigerians did during the oil boom era.

The leadership of Nigeria must learn to help others while helping themselves hence they must enjoy today with 10% (ten percent) and keep 90% (ninety percent) for the future of Nigerians.

The notion to call any nation a success is -- stable and healthy. Stable meaning stability, stability in transfer of powers, stability in the due process of the law and stability in democracy. ---- Healthy meaning economic health, economic health means economic progress, economic health means strength.

There should and must be a sweeping renewal in Nigeria for her citizen to rededicate themselves for the future of Nigeria. Rather than reacting in fear for the future good of Nigeria, we must all react in faith and believe that the best is yet to come.

Instead of a tragedy such as economic mismanagement and lack of leadership with compassion to tear the nation apart, it should bring the country together. This must be a lesson for communities to come together.

The federal government has neglected the nation's poorest people at a time when economic hardship is destroying the country. The federal government must create social, political and economic reforms for the poor people of Nigeria.

Every President or Head-Of-State should know that there comes a time, when one should step aside. The seat of the Presidency should not become a personal property of one individual or one ethnic group.

The leader of any nation must have a vision for that country --- a vision of a strong and prosperous nation. The implementation of this vision by the leader, must be with extreme compassion so as to give hope (not despair) to the citizens regardless of which ethnic group is on the throne of leadership.

Nigeria is fast becoming a country where you can not really call one citizen belonging to one ethnic group because most of them are a mixture of various ethnic groups and ethnic backgrounds.

All Nigerians should strive for peace and harmony with each other, There is no longer North, South, East or West because of so many intermarriages. We should all be Nigerians first and foremost. Ethnic groups have crossed lines and joined into one another hence there is no need nor any reason for violence and hatred on ethnic differences, we must not turn Nigeria into another Rwanda or Bosnia.

A President develops attitudes, even emotions that are expressed through the actions of his cabinet members. The President or Head-Of-State must create goodwill, establish trust and form good relationship with the citizens of the entire country regardless of what ethnic group is the presumed majority. It must also be made known to every President or Head-Of-State that he lives two lives, one of his own and the other one on the lips of others.

In the country today, all the ingredients for a long-term crime epidemic remain in place; massive unemployment, a huge gap between the rich and the poor, a proliferation of guns and a police force that is ill-equipped, underpaid and under compensated. With all these in mind, one wonders if the forces of order can contain the forces of disorder.

Nigeria today is a place where the Igbo's own the economy, the Hausa's run the politics, the Yoruba's run the educational structure, while the Ijaws who are the fourth largest tribe and the prime producers of oil, runs nothing and also have nothing but mass poverty amidst all the riches the Ijaws produce for the country.

Nigeria needs a leader who will be indispensable, a leader who can calm the fears of the North and temper the hopes of the South. A leader who cares much about the strength and future greatness of Nigeria, not a leader who only cares for material wealth so much so that he is willing to do anything to enrich himself while the rest of the nation relish in poverty, that is why most protest today, you never know if the protest is politically motivated or economically motivated.

To avoid all the blood-letting that is going on, the North and the South should negotiate for quiet transfer of power, the

North should abdicate enough power to co-opt enough Southerners to leadership positions especially that of the Presidency because the North should realize that they could no longer control the masses alone.

Nigerian military leaders have always wielded an abundance of power and privileges. Nigeria's military leaders exercise supreme authority over foreign and defense matters, the military leadership can dissolve his cabinet and government at will and enjoys a regal status very far above the law that he never has to worry about being impeached or compelled to resign.

The federal government (under military or civilian) must prove to be fiscally prudent and investor-friendly. It has to reject punitive taxation of the rich. It has to get a handle on criminal violence.

The military reign in Nigeria has left much of the population disenchanted with the ruling class and dispirited by the big erosion of living standard. The ultimate leader of Nigeria must diminish the gap between the rich and the poor.

The Nigerian population are not looking to choose a governing majority but they want to select the person most qualified to banish all illusions, to overcome the divisions and unite the entire country.

High-rates of joblessness has fomented a climate of seething social discontent with students, workers and human rights advocates staging strikes or street marches to protest their bleak fortunes.

Nigerians no longer cared about ideologies but they want dynamic leadership that would create jobs, promote togetherness, maintain political stability and preserve social protections.

Most leaders the country has had till date have always behaved like aristocrats, unmoved by the poor's plight. Any emerging leader, who wants the Presidency, must remind the people of Nigeria, not only of Nigeria's glorious past (of the oil boom era) but must also demonstrate that Nigeria is in touch with the present economic predicament and is preparing leadership for the future.

Nigeria's economic problems are temporary, Nigeria is still strong, still vibrant and still vital not only in African affairs but in world affairs.

There is no doubt that to survive and thrive in today's competitive environment, people must adapt, evolve and diversify. Nigeria needs strong leadership today to solve tomorrow's problems. It is very obvious, you can not wait for the future to come to you, you have to build the future for yourself by making leadership visions become reality. To achieve this, you need energetic and innovative leaders with insight to make it happen. Leaders that know that if you can prevent it today you do not have to pay for it tomorrow.

Recently, despite great strides toward educational convergence, Southerners wage and employment trends have been generally negative, relative to those of Northerners. For Southerners overall and for young Southerners in particular, wage and labor market participation declines have been severe.

Nigerians definitely can not change the past, but with strong, dynamic and able leadership, the country can take control of the future because when the country needs performance, nothing is more important than the performers -- good leadership.

Adopting new ideologies is no simple task. It takes foresight, courage, creative thinking and a lot of teamwork. The rewards ultimately are well worth the sacrifice and effort.

For a while, Nigeria maintained strong leadership role in sub-saharan Africa, however, a record alone is not enough to ensure continued success. Ultimate success requires strong vision. Nigerians must share a vision for the future. A vision that challenges all Nigerians to break through traditional boundaries, to integrate and refocus capabilities and to develop depth of talent for the long term not the short term of pleasures and long term miseries.

Nigerians must know that real economic growth has to be driven by the private sector not the federal government. The only solution to Nigeria's problems is self-help. The type of good democracy that one expects in Nigeria will fail woefully if the private sector with the full support of the federal government can not alleviate poverty.

No human being will follow a leader anywhere unless that leader is absolutely committed to the journey and its destination. Most Nigerians do not care very much about ideology, military or democratic leadership. Most Nigerians are concerned about food on the table. Any leader that is not committing himself or herself with this issue is not fulfilling the needs of the masses.

The federal government and the private sector must help workers boost their skills. Most of the things we see today in the political life of Nigeria, is a grave consequence of economic stress. It is the insecurity and lack of hope that brings out the violent side of the poor masses.

In Nigeria, today, people are living in one of those very remarkable times in history when two crucial elements for societal change are in existence -- 1. new values and 2. economic hardship. Historically, you can not have just one element to affect change, you must have both elements. One of the elements is not strong enough to produce societal change. There must be a confluence of both new values and economic hardship to affect change. This is precisely what is happening now in Nigeria.

People are more productive if they are treated with respect. Nigerians do not want an authoritarian government, they want a government that respects the people, the people they govern and a government that offers its people a chance to grow personally.

The Nigerian people and the mass media are very effective at discovering and communicating problems but solutions are rarely discovered or talked about. I do believe that if you are not part of the solution you are definitely part of the problem. Also, in my humble opinion, the federal government has to realize that the Nigerian people will make or break the country hence the government must be nice to her people and recognize the fact that it is commitment not authority that produces results.

The government must treat the old people with respect rather than being chuckled into early retirement, they should be considered a valuable resource and offered part-time or consulting jobs.

Nigerians must show the kind of foresight that is rare in most nations, Nigeria should not just respond to change, Nigeria should anticipate change. Change is hard but change is ultimately good.

Most times, the source of vision is a leader, a person who possesses a unique combination of skills; 1. the mental power to create a vision and 2. the practical ability to bring the vision into reality. Nigeria needs a leader with a vision to carry the nation into the 21st century.

To be successful, a leader must create forceful vision of a desired state of affairs. Successful leaders see themselves as leaders not micro or macro managers. A leader should be concerned about the nation's existence, its general direction and doing the right thing. A leader must be a visionary. Logic is not everything. The simple idea is that by envisioning the future you want, you can easily achieve your goal. Vision is the link between dream and action. The President must see himself as a leader not just head of state.

Well-informed strategies alone will not motivate the Nigerian people. Only a leader with a real mission or sense of purpose that comes out of spiritual dimension will capture the hearts of the masses.

Vision is practical as well as mystical. It is easier to get from point a to point b if you know where point b is and how to recognize it when you arrive at point b.

Without a goal, neither a country nor her people will get to the 21st century with success. People who have a vision are motivated to make it a reality. Creating the vision is the leader's first role, next, the leader must attract people who can help realize it by adopting the vision as their own and sharing responsibility for achieving the vision.

When people identify with their country's purpose, when people experience ownership in a shared vision, they find themselves with great confidence. Once people experience ownership in a leader's vision, the leader's job has just begun. The leader must then reinforce, refocus and refine the vision while supporting and inspiring the people aligned with the vision.

Leadership emerges naturally when the leader attracts followers. Objectives are set by those who must make the objectives happen and that is the job of a leader with a vision.

Every President or Head-Of-State must realize that the role of a leader is a servant's role. The leader should be a teacher, a coach, a mentor, a developer of human potential, a team builder not controller of people. A leader's role is, supporting his people and running interference for his people.

The federal government must know that freedom and respect for the individual are the best motivators for the masses. The leaders of Nigeria today should be determined that the children must have better education and more of everything. The only way to achieve this goal is for leadership to sacrifice for the children what they lacked.

America's greatest strength is people, well educated, ethnically diverse and full confidence to achieve economic success. Nigeria is also blessed with great people, well educated people and ethnically diverse but are not confident to achieve economic success due to lack of able leadership with a vision.

The wisdom, judgement and experience of older people are invaluable to the nation. They are a vital future manpower resource. Some countries are taking the lead that many will follow -- they are rehiring the workers who have retired.

The nation's competitive edge is people- an educated, skilled work force that is eager to develop its potent human potential while contributing to the nation's growth.

The leaders of Nigeria are free to stop justifying their failures and they should move ahead and ask themselves, where do we go from here? which way Nigeria? left, right or center?

Thinking is the ability to synthesize and make generalizations, to divide into categories to draw inferences, to distinguish between opinion and fact, to put facts in order to analyze a problem. Thinking has to do with the way information is arranged and rearranged to make decisions, create opportunities, solve problems and raise human potentials.

Thinking is the most fundamental and important skill that a leader must have. Like all human skills, thinking can be learned and developed. Nigerian leaders need to learn how to learn, you can adapt and change, no matter what technological, social or economic interchange occur. If you know how to learn, you will not be completely ravaged when in need of change. If you know how to learn, you have the necessary tool; your ability to learn, to study new fields and acquire new knowledge. Learning requires openness and curiosity.

Nigerian leaders should be open-minded and should be curios about learning and thinking for a vision for the country because learning is a continuous process, you only stop learning when you die. Learning how to learn requires modesty, you have to be able to concede to learn.

In every major urban area, there should be at least some association between schools and businesses around them. This must reflect knowledgeable self-interest by companies that realize that their futures are tied to having proportionately trained and healthy manpower. The federal government should grow more and more supportive of

75

education and educators should be wisely promoting all kinds of new partnerships between businesses and the schools. Nigerian businesses should be contributing to the schools in their area by giving money, grants, and scholarships.

Business leaders must realize that if their companies are to prosper, their surrounding communities must flourish also. A community can only be healthy as its schools. Companies should adopt a school in their community.

The adopt-a-school is easy. Rather than contributing to education in a perplexed way, individual establishments have to link up with specific schools in their community and elsewhere to propagate a personal relationship based on the schools needs. If we do not save the conditions of schools today, it will corrode the quality of life in Nigeira. Schools and companies should work out exceptional relationships based on local community needs and resources.

Companies should donate computers, scientific equipment to colleges, universities, secondary schools and primary schools. Computer skills and scientific breakthroughs are the keys to the future of Nigeria.

When everything is said and done, one of the bottom line is that, illiteracy is a key factor to the multimillion Naira cost of keeping people in prision. Half of the prision population of Nigeria is illeterate. Obviously, there is a direct comparison between illiteracy and unemployment.

Companies in Nigeria must join in the fight against illiteracy. Business (i.e. the private sector) should be committed to upgrading the quality of education in Nigeria, by donating generously.

Nigerian corporations are in a position to make huge

donations to Nigeria's schools. There is great need for businesses to share in the educational needs of the entire country.

Nigerian corporations have to act on the basis of the interconnectedness between people and profit. What this means is that corporate interests and the interests of the people and the communities must be the same.

Nigeria is rich in ethnic groups. The richer the mix in ethnicity, the more the creative, hence Nigeria must take adventage of her ethnic mix.

In Nigeria, we have not yet begun to develop the real potent potential of fantastic mix of people. To reach our full potential as individuals and as a nation, we need a vision and a visioner. Nigerians must be ready to make a commitment to a pupose, a goal, a vision that is bigger than themselves -- big enough to make them stretch and grow until they assume personal responsibility for achieving it.

Whatever your country's vision, you know it is effective when people in the country take personal responsibility for achieving it. You have to believe in the power of one individual to change history, to change your community or simply to change another person's life for the better.

If Nigerian economy continues a downward trend and the people continue to be hopeless and spirits of the people remain undernourished, internal conflicts will continue to endanger security and social status of the nation.

People must be given the right tools of opportunity --- education, healthcare, legal/constitutional rights and political participation -- these tools will help people to better able to make the right choices in their lives. With these tools, they can lift themselves out of poverty, they can and must also lift their families, communities and most importantly the nation.

Against political, social and huge economic odds, Nigerians must transform their lives. Nigerians must strive to overcome poverty, illiteracy, inadequate health care and improve the circunstances of the masses.

Crime has taking a dramatic upswing across Nigeria as rising unemployment and economic hardship drive Nigerians to acts of increasing desperation to obtain money in any way they can imagine.

The crime problem was intensified by the economic downward trend and it is likely to get worse before it gets better. The federal government has a huge task of convincing wary foreign investors that Nigeria is worthy of continued investment, even while the country gains a world-wide reputation for high-level corruption, instability and exalting lawlessness.

Stories of sophisticated political crimes, armed robberies, illegal/illicit drug trafficking and petty thefts have come to dominate the front pages of Nigerian newspaper so much that, the masses now distrust the political landscape of the entire federal government.

Robberies and acts of armed violence since the economic slump have reached their highest level in more than a decade. A combination of economic, social and cultural factors are contributing to the problem.

Nigeria is witnessing not just economic problems but also moral devaluation. Some workers are turning to crime because their pay is low. This paints a grim picture of widespread unrest in the country. It is a very very sad situation for a country whose future looked so bright since the oil boom days, more than sad, it is becoming dangerous.

Nigerian politics for some time now is a competition among branches of the economy especially oil, agriculture, the military institution and the banks. People who have reached the top of their profession in these branches of the economy are the ones vying for political leadership and the competition is very rigid. The competition is more ideological, since the profitable branches of economy --- oil, banking and agriculture have interest in ensuring a class warfare.

The oil money that floated the Nigerian governments and still keeps much of Nigeria afloat is decreasing everyday. Eventually, only openness to foreign investment and political stability will help the nation.

The military institution prefers leadership by decrees. The military, it seem has a lot of clout due to their possession of weaponry and vast workforce that can not be discarded without risking social explosion.

To achieve political stability, Nigerians must believe in the principles of non-violence and the need to uplift the poorest and the needy members of the nation first.

Nigeria's economy must and should be based on agriculture because a nation that can not feed itself and also export food is not ready for the 21st century. Nigerians need a better understanding of the problems of poor people and the strengths of poor people. The government and community leaders must take care of the people at the bottom or else the top will fall.

People must volunteer to help the helpless, people must

volunteer to make a change in society. You can donate your time in an average of six hours a week for a cause you believe in to make a difference.

Blaming others will not solve our problems. The Nigerian society can not be stable or prosperous if Nigeria continue to produce the big disparity between the rich and the poor and between the well-educated and less-educated.

The continuing religious turmoil between christians and muslim in Nigeria must stop. The nation's leadership must devise a strategy to bring people of all faiths together. A healthy nation-wide discourse aimed at finding solutions to all the problems confronting the nation should begin immediately. Leadership must give hope and encouragement.

The poor people of Nigeria have made enough sacrifices, it is now time for the rich and political elite of the country to make some of the sacrifices, it is time for the elite to give back to the country what they got from the country.

After years of terror, curfews, military sieges, death and the resulting collapse of the country's oil-based economy, the citizens of Nigeria are fed up. They condemn a government they do not trust and are disgusted of a political movement that has been infiltrated by tribalists that are more interested in extorting money than winning a cause.

Nigerians are always concerned with the values of their leaders and the qualities of leadership, integrity, intellect and character but Nigerians must also remember that every saint has a past and every sinner has a future. Talk is cheap, it is performance that counts. It is one thing to critcize   and blame others, it is quite another thing to govern.

The messenger is as important as the message. He or she

must be personable, articualte and self-deprecating. His or her message must be affirmation and optimism.

A leader that is weak is not a leader that can lead. You have to believe in the power of one individual to change history, to change your community or simply to change another person's life for the better. People must ask themselves, what does it mean to be a Nigeiran?

A chief of state (President or Head-Of-State) requires a stature to unify the country and represent the country before the world. Nigeria needs presidential action on the economy and political stability. The President as a leader is expected to make policy not perform miracles.

There are two halves of the Presidency -- 1. chief of state and 2. head of government. A leader must have features such as vision, intelligence and commitment. The other qualities a leader must have are; consensus building, interactive style, comfort with uncertainty and the sharing of power and information.

Northerners hold most of the positions of authority in most workplaces in the country. In profound numbers, Southerners make up the greatest underutilized class and the largest pool of untapped leadership potentials in the country. More than 90 percent (90%) of top government positions are held by Northerners. The leadership, insinuates that either there are very few Southerners deserving of holding such positions or qualified Southerners are ignored. The nation has a large cadre of well-educated, experienced professional Southerners.

The leadership has always had its hands on the throat of the oil-dominated federal budget and the people have absolutely no control over what happens with the money, all

81

this is due to lack of accountability.

The future of Nigeria belongs to those who build not to those who destroy. We need to nurture and teach the children of Nigeria, it is a community job that should involve more than schools, teacher and parents. Children of Nigeria need people to reach out to them.

The country (Nigeria) must have the ability to attract, retain and motivate individuals through compensation plans to people, for their individual job performance. This is an historical moment when dignity and civility are at a very low ebb in Nigeria. Nigerians and the government should wake up now and salvage the nation. A government with compasision is what Nigeians are looking for.

The personal needs of poor people -- adequate food, housing and finalcial support for themselves and their families are often neglected, ignored or shrugged off by the government. Lack of housing and the struggle to keep up with the cost of living has contributed to serious crime problems. Providing a decent quality of life for poor people is critical and crucial in today's society by any government. What Nigeria needs today is solutions not criticism.

POLITICAL STRUCTURE

Politics in Nigeria is in-built with personality cult, elitist in conduct and ethnic oriented. The political structure is also built from the top downward instead of from the bottom to the top. The leadership must give equal rights to all Nigerians for equal participation in the political process regardless of their ethnic background, wealth, socio-political background, professional endeavors and most important their religion.

Nigerians must see politics as a game not a war that must be won at all cost. Party politics or any politics at all must and should be issue-oriented. Any politics must also have trust and tolerance.

Most Southerners instead of striving and dying for a political agenda would rather be satisfied with immediate monetary gains and future monetary promises. Most Southerners are really not politicians they are business oriented. The people who study politics, play politics and understand politics are the Northerners. All political appointments in the country has been based on religion and ethnicity not competency. Due to the unequal participation of politics in the country, most conflicts in the South is over money while in the North all conflicts are due to religion.

The Northerners thrive on politics because they get lucrative contracts as assistance. The Northerners are the most politically conscious people in the country. They are not industrially oriented like the Igbos, they are not into manufacturing like the Yorubas. The Northerner view politics as the means to their political and economic existence in Nigeria.

83

Nigeria has gone from a nation being led by people with vision (Gowon, Awolowo, Azikiwe and Balewa) to being led by caretakers -- people who force their way into leadership only to enrich themselves and their cronies. No more vision for the greatness of the nation only a vision for individual accumulation of wealth.

A good rule of life is that you learn more from your defeats and failures than from your victories and successes. In Nigeria, however, such education has been very costly, which is why Nigeria should learn from other nation's defeats, failures and economic woes.

Nigerian leadership must plan, finance and install modern transportation, power generation (huge electrification projects) and communication systems capable of sustaining the blistering growth of the future.

Nigeria has an enormous need for new electric power generation. With all the difficulties Nigeria need to overcome and all the rewards Nigeria has to gain -- this is the time to build more power generation plants instead of the proliferation of small house-hold generators in every house that can afford to buy one. Nigeria Electric Power Authority (NEPA)'s budget should be increased and more power plants built. If this is achieved, it will eradicate the disgraceful scenario whereby even when a President or Head-Of-State is hosting a ceremony, the thought of NEPA's electricity power failure is always impending. Although Nigeria has a reputation for political instability hence foreign investors are hesitant in investing in the country but more of a huge problem is electricity consumption. The federal government-owned NEPA has been unable to keep up with demand. The nation must privatize NEPA.

The emergence of small/big power generators in homes

everywhere in the country is so ludicrous it is astounding. Everywhere you go, there is a power generator even in State House Ribadu Road (alias Doban Barracks) and the Presidential Mansion in Abuja.

This is not an era of specialization. Everything now is about cross-fertilization. We must diversify our economy, most important -- agriculture is the way to prosperity.

Making our communities better and stronger takes commitment. A leader must be strong on ideas and must not be weak on administrative skills. A leader must have moral vision.

In the political arena, what Southerners are really after is not only legal rights but full acceptance into the mainstream of Nigerian society and this acceptance is only granted or restrained by the so-called majority at its approbation. If Southerners must be accepted, they must also be welcomed with open arms. It is not easy to change the hearts and minds of millions of Northerners but we must start from one point to the other. Southerners should stop feeling sorry for themselves, they may be victims but they should come together and care for each other. The common topic of all this is simply facing the facts, working to bring out the best in ourselves and offering something worthy to the Northerners and the entire nation.

The political movements in the South have become more inclined on filing grievances than on promoting economic opportunities.

In a Presidential election, organization and early political work are more important to a challenger than to an incumbent for whom the central voting question is whether the nation wants to continue his or her policies and leadership or switch roads. Above all, the personal and the public life of a leader must cast light on the achievements of community improvements. Dealing extensively with the cultural and political background of a leader is also crucial and the federal government should be interested in finding ways to help people who are financially deprived.

A leader must be a defender of the downtrodden. A leader must have solidarity with all victims of injustice. Any Nigerian leader must certainly be aware of the inner contradictions between the past and the future of Nigeria.

The chance for personal fulfillment among Southern Nigerians, even survival for some, can only come with political liberty. All Nigerians regardless of ethnic background should be expected to fulfill some great destiny in the service of the Nigerian people.

Considering the chaos of their childhood, it is no small accomplishment that most Southerners survived to adulthood. Today, most rich Southerners are those who could not enjoy eating unless they see someone who is hungry.

There are mostly three stages in the life of a self-made man; 1. the acquisitive stage, 2. the contemplative stage and 3. the distributive stage. These three stages also belong to a self-reliant country. The acquisitive stage for a self-reliant country is the stage where the country discovers her mineral resources and human potentials, while the contemplative stage is the stage where the leaders contemplate the future of the country and the potential stability of the nation. The distributive stage, is the stage where the wealth of the nation is distributed equally to the states and her people for the ultimate benefit of the entire country.

You have to give people training in education, give

people opportunities and most of all give people a bright future. As politicians increasingly shout and growl at each other in private and public jurisdictions, do they realize that children are listening? Everyone should be aware that children not only listen to adults, they actively emulate adults. Leaders must teach by example, the values of social order. Leaders must show the suitable form of civil conversation and political modulation by their conduct and demeanor in and out of politics and government.

Nigerian children and the entire populace solicit frantically for better leadership examples, instead, leaders are fighting each other, it is very dazzling in politics. In Nigerian politics today, sour declamation is driving out reasoned discussion.

Nigerians (either in politics or in the military) should strive intrepidly to teach and practice civility, democracy and rational conversation. Politics should not be the territory of hateful language, polarized debate and furious feats. Nigerians must build and re-build our sense of self-restraint and above all, our social responsibility. We must realize that what happened in the country can not be changed but we must learn from it and see what good we can do and what good we can give to our society.

A leader must be a person who is kind, loving and cares about others, not a person who goes to church or mosque every week and looks down on the others because they do not live the life of a Christian or Muslim. A leader must act by doing good deeds for others.

Nigeria needs innovators -- men and women whose ideas and leadership will improve Nigerian schools, businesses and government. Nigeria needs reform and hope for a better future. Nigeria needs born leaders -- leaders who are poised and outgoing with a wide winning smile. We need leaders who are original thinkers, leaders who will make their living based on the originality of their minds.

The leadership of Nigeria must set a commission that will do a one-year study that will look at ways to root out government waste because we have to find creative solutions to our problems.

The widening gap between the rich and the poor in Nigeria is excruciating. The richest 10% (ten percent) of Nigerian house-holds now own more than 90% (ninety percent) of it's wealth, with the result that Nigeria is the most economically stratified nation in the developing world.

The leadership must know that ambition translate into achievement. The leaders must be determined and leave nothing to chance. The achievers paradox is that, you have a better chance of winning if winning is not the only reason that you are in the political game.

There is a big difference in where a person began in life compared with where a person ended up. Your efforts must justify your achievement and your achievement must justify your rewards. The achievers thinking: From a position of power he or she must do more good in the world. Leaders should have a cause they dedicate their lives to beyond their own private interests. Nigerian leaders must know that the comfort of their future life depends upon their present conduct.

The distance between poor Southerners and affluent Northerners has widened into an ethnic chasm. In the political arena, the sentiment has proved a breeding ground for ethnic suspicion. In Nigeria, there is a sense of ethnic identification with leaders. When the leadership is bad, it is excruciating for Southerners and it is causing paranoia and conspiracy thinking.

Nigeria's ethnic-based politics and leadership poses central questions -- does a split along ethnic-linguistic lines invite anachy and ultimately the disintegration of one of the world's largest oil producing nations? Or does acknowledging ethnic disputes defuse tensions and ultimately draw together a nation that for years has been at odds with itself. But one of the most ludicrous aspects of Nigeria is that the people lack a tradition of political tolerance among its ethnic groups. Since Nigeria's independence, each government, be it military or civilian has imprisoned or killed thousands of opponents.

Nigerians must be able to get beyond what divides Nigerians. Nigerians must stop embracing ethnic politics. Nigerians can only have political stability and live in a free society where they have rights, where they can critize their government without fear of being locked-up, killed or look over their shoulder. People should participate in the political process regardless if they win or lose. People must realize that, just because you do not win does not mean you are not in the political game.

Every leader should pledge and work hard to revive the dying agricultural sector of the economy and slash defense spending. Increasing spending should be on education, money for roads and bridges should be multiplied.

Production of oil --- Nigeria's major bread earner, has nose-dived, but defense spending has continuosly swallowed the federal budget, you can barely trace the percentage of the budget that goes to social services.

The poorest regions in the country have yet to receive

89

adequate resources to match the regions that have been strongest educationally.

The country needs better schools, better health care, more investments to boost agricultural production and most of all political stability. Politics based on ethnicity is dangerous. Equality is what the people need not segregation. Decisions should be made and compromises should be reached based on fair play and equality both on domestic and international issues. Nigerians must stop putting their ethnicity first. You must be a Nigerian first. People in Nigeria are mostly concerned only about their own language or resources and culture, the other ethnic groups they feel do not count.

The leaders of Nigeria and the Nigerian people can not change the past but they must do everything within their power to change the future. Nigerians want better life, food, jobs, water, light, housing, good roads and adequate communication network.

The best defense is always a good offense. As a leader you can not be too quick to solve political conflicts through force, there must be peaceful negotiation and resolutions first.

Too many people in Nigeria are expecting too many things for nothing. The federal government could not and will not solve all problems. Private business and individual sacrifice and spending will help solve problems.

The old leaders should step aside and allow Nigeria to have new leadership. Nigeria needs leaders with energy and new ideas, leaders who can speak out for those who need strong support.

As a leader, a politician must have the vision to take

Nigeria into the next century and ethnicity has to be left behind and it should have been left behind decades ago.

Leaders must understand the might of political power and get results. Leaders must be experts at understanding and using political power. Leadership -- strong and good is the only way to make Nigeria a better country, I do not care if it is military or civilian as long as it is the same result -- a better Nigeria for all.

No matter how good you are in Nigeria, if you are a Southerner, you have a harder time being fairly rewarded for your skill and effort but at the same time, most Southerners like to see their fellow Southerner in hardship.

Too often, people identify problems in the country but they do not challenge themselves to think of solutions. Keep in mind, that once you identify a need or a problem you must find an elegant solution.

Politics or government can accomplish a lot with a good leader, a leader that has the willingness to admit mistakes, a leader who is different and a leader who is ready to make a great difference.

Authority has almost vanished in the country, people do not respect authority any more, they only fear guns. Authority which is vested in figures from the President on down and in institutions. Nigeria needs a man or a woman of unimpeachable authority. Nigerians must respect authority, be it the President, teacher or police man.

People live by rules because they are rules, because these rules give the community shape, coherence and a shared view-point and make them feel worthy of the rewards they are promised. Decades ago, Nigeria is a rules-following society, it was a culture of desires not obligation.

The present Nigerian leaders have mortgaged the future of Nigeria's children with decay and incompetence. The present Nigerian leaders should sober up, walk out of the back room of North/South isolationism, defeat, hatred and ethnic based politics. The present leadership should promote peace terms generous to winner and loser alike and realize that helping others truly is the way to happiness.

Money and power do not teach us moral lessons or make us better citizens, they only enrich our all too brief lives by investing each moment with the highest quality. Oil boom which flourished decades ago, was testaments of hope for the future and wonder at the miracles it most assuredly would bring. The theme that dominated this period was spend, spend, spend, spend, spend, no investment, no future plans. The mood with which they spend was one of impatience and over confidence. If we must learn from our mistakes and accept responsibility, Nigerians must not lose the capacity for respect, difference and trust. Nigerians must now have faith in their destiny and confidence in their future.

At this time, when the leaders of Nigeria are held in low regard, the country is yearning for leaders with discipline, dedication, integrity and principle.

Through money and power we may not live longer but we can live better, more intensely. It is not the fruit of experience that matters but experience itself is the end.

In the botched elections between the Social Democratic Party (S.D.P.) and the National Republican Convention (N.R.C.), It was astounding to find the involvement of past political/military leaders. Leaders like, retired General Yakubu Gowon who ruled Nigeria for nine years and led a three-year-old civil war to victory and was deposed in a coup for alleged mass corruption in 1975. Another potent surprise in the democratic process was the entrance of Ojukwu, the former Nigerian Army colonel who led the civil war in eastern Nigeria after breaking away from the federation in 1967 and was head of the rebel republic of Biafra.

Nigeria that is great, a Nigeria that will be greater with our hard work and sacrifice that is what we should be striving for as Nigerians. Nigeria must honor people who have followed their dreams and are an inspiration to others because hard work has its rewards.

One of the most impressive adventures of Nigeria today is the rapidly burgeoning interpenetration of ethnicity and cultures.

The Nigerian populace, especially in the South are tired of being terrorized by law enforcement agents. Everyone's perceptions are affected by circumstances. Any mind that is enlarged to a new idea never returns to its preceding enormity. Nigeria is desperately in need for change, also security and welfare is of the utmost concern. Nigerians should stop existing and start living.

It is universally true, that it is possible to be both a good reporter and a good human being, hence one would like to see accurate reporting with facts and balanced reporting at all times without undermining the security of the nation and respect for freedom of speech with internal editing.

Recently, Nigeria's discussions of crime and punishment have been snared by a culture of rage and ignorance, guided mostly not by reason or compassion but by prejudice, based on ethnic background and revenge. There are enormous contradictions that make it difficult in Nigeria to understand the issues of guilt and innocence, personal responsibility and societal obligations. Nigerian judiciary system criss-cross between two extremes, conferring too much absolutions on some people (the rich and the Northerners) and too much guilt on others (the poor and Southerners). Nigeria has become a society in which citizens fear one another so much so that they perpetuate the conditions in which violence continues unabated.

Nigeria does not have a single program on crime prevention, rehabilitation of criminals and the idea that society bears much responsibility for criminal behavior.

Since independence, terror and hope alternately grip Nigeria but much of the future of the nation depends on the political skills and vision of the leadership. Nigeria needs a pragmatic leader. Past leaders of Nigeria are tainted with ethnic violence and bloodshed and the future leaders too are unpredictable.

Collective punishment of people in the South only harms the innocent not the guilty people and this drives people to more violence and revenge syndrome. It is time for Nigerians, North and South to accept each other as one without inherited seeds of hatred.

Religions must co-exist in a unified ONE Nigeria. No single Nigerian should be scared of intimidation by weapons because in any religion, Christian or Muslim -- faith is the most potent weapon. Nigerians should have faith in oneness and be compassionate to one another.

For a while now, Nigeria has abdicated its historic leadership role in sub-saharan Africa, this has created a vacuum that is immediately filled by South Africa. Nigeria's leadership role has been reduced in influence, participation and persuasion in African and world affairs.

In Nigeria, there are many factors for instability, not just coups and counter-coups. There are thousands of unemployed youths who are university graduates, mostly in the South. There are unemployed peasants who have surged from the villages into the capital cities of their states of origin in search of jobs. Also there are thousands of retrenched workers who were laid-off from government parastatals.

In Nigeria today, corruption is so very much entrenched in every facet of the society it is scandalous. The system no longer works, everybody wants something for nothing, everyone enriches themselves through whatever position they occupy, be it messenger, clerk or managing director or military General. No matter what the leadership (either military or civilian) says, it can not fundamentally fight corruption because doing so might harm its own entire interest -- and that is its grip on power perpetually.

Nigeria is a much troubled nation where poverty, religious in-fighting and ethnic based politics and leadership has wiped the smile off people's faces and draped the cities, coasts and villages in a mantle of despair. Instead of the dreary streets, poverty and despair that is apparent everywhere, what is needed is buoyant optimism, a look of prosperity and colorfully vibrant streets in every major city in Nigeria.

Throughout every military administration, the military leadership has kept Northern politicians in majority power. Although animosities obviously linger since the Major Kaduna Enzeaogu's coup, the North and South should link into ONE great Nigeria and lead this great nation into prosperity.

Each consecutive administration has pumped substantial funds into public housing and other development projects in the North. Also every administration has made it a priority to neglect developments in all the oil producing areas. As of now, the entire military in Nigeria is overwhelmingly populated by the Northerners.

The politics of oil makes for strange bedfellows. A person has to have financial resources in order to achieve financial success. Ultimately, you must use your harvest to help the needy.

While saving money is a basic component of a responsible lifestyle, no one becomes wealthy by savings alone. People become wealthy by earning. Your earning power is far greater than your saving power in the road that leads to wealth. Nigerians must remember it is not just how fast you can go, it is also where you are going.

The situation of Nigeria today is a testament to excesses of the oil boom era and a classic example of losing touch with the entire public. Clearly, one of the motivating factors in the downturn of economic and political events today in the country is greed. You have people trying to make a fast Naira. Leaders in Nigeria need to come up with a clear economic message that connects with the poor masses and the middle class who feel they are under a great assault.

Population growth has outstripped food production. The situation looks gloomy at the moment but the prospects for avoiding long-term haul is encouraging. Many of the problems Nigeria faces today as a nation concerns not only the economy but the national character.

Over time, the commonality of interests will become apparent to both the North and the South, although right now, that clearly has not happened at this moment in the nation's politics.

The leadership, be it military or civilian, must bring itself to respect significant differences of opinion and remain tolerant to variances from the government message on issues. Instead of leaders polarizing the South and the North, they should unite them. Leaders must have the political will and the administrative skill to enforce change. There is no action without consequence, and no pleasure without pain.

Nigerian workers are prepared and motivated to work harder when they know that the federal government and management listens to their suggestions. Workers are very eager to have a greater voice in the operations of their government and their companies.

Nobody in Nigeria should care who run things (military or civilians) as long as they run them efficiently and effectively.

Good business means giving back. Politics as much as military rationale have tended to determine what gets funded in the country. Over the years, the military provides a window on a corner of the defense budget where the interest of contractors eager for business and the armed forces units desparate for new equipment and political representatives ready to favor their constituents have merged.

Violence makes people to resist change. If you are born with great pride, you also have great responsibility. There should be more conversation between the leaders in the South and the North and less combat. It is time to erase suspicion and fear, it is time to look to the future with cooperation and unity.

Most political aggrandizement is an issue related to poverty. Nigerians should look for a brighter future rather than a bleak past. Reconciliation with the enemy does not come easy but it is better for the future. Nigerians must choose between dialogue and grave devastation.

No matter where an idea comes from, it should not be Southern idea or a Northern idea, nor should it be a military idea or a political idea, it should be a good Nigerian idea that is good for the future of the nation.

Nigeria is a nation that has been graced by success. Both Southern and Northern Nigerians must realize that the marriage of two fortunes makes for a bigger fortune. The bigger the company the cheaper the cost and the bigger the profit. Power is nothing without control and sharing. We cannot have a non-political solution to a political issue. Being a leader means being the best and setting the standards.

If Nigeria must succeed in an economic revolution, the country and her citizens (especially the leaders) must be free-minded and defend policies that will enable the country to achieve economic prosperity once again and everyone should be willing to pay the price today for the future benefits.

The leadership and every Nigerian citizen must bring confidence in the nation to restore shaken investor confidence in Nigeria which has been mired in economic and political uncertainty.

Leaders in the country must take leadership roles in negotiating, compromising and working to build fences that will bring the country into one entity.

The only way to have a clear indication of political stability and maturity in any system of government is the willingness of political differences and rivalry to be in the open and for compromise to exist in every realm of political dealings.

Conflicting views must exist in any political setting but exchange of views must not be prevented. Exchange of views are the vehicle for growth and progress in any nation.

The prospect of Nigeria is bright and promising but an overwhelming majority of Nigerian people are skeptical about the wisdom of government policies.

If the military or the politicians are to gain respect they must do good to the nation and for her citizens and they must show that they can also govern. People naturally tend to seek to participate in political decision-making.

The events in Nigeria today are devastating. People do not have compassion any longer. In the name of state/national security, the government and the people are visiting terror upon one another. Through all this time Nigeria remain well into the next decade her own worst enemy.

One of the reasons why people are clamoring for political leadership is because democracy, at its best, allows more voices to be heard than any other form of government. Everybody wants to join in the exchange of ideas. Unlike in a military regime where whatever you say or do, if it is not in favor of the military administration, you are regarded as state security risk and you might be shot or locked-up for the entire tenure of the military administration.

Every administration should know that worthy innovations come from a variety of places and we cannot afford the risk of being deprived of anyone's contribution to the betterment of the nation. Ascertaining that every Nigerian has a decent chance in life is very much in the self-interest of any government.

Since independence, while ordinary Nigerians search aimlessly for the most basic necessities of life, the privileged few are on cue for whatever they need. The political elite and the senior military elite and their children, all they really know how to do best is consume and destroy, not build and transfer.

Nothing is more decisive for Nigeria than the successful conduct of its internal relations. There should be broad based agreement that national security and national safety could best be assured through empowerment. Nigeria's major plan should be economic revolution aimed at political reconstruction. A well-fed citizen and a stable nation will secure Nigeria peace and ultimately good friendship of all nations because it is in the interest of nations to have Nigeria as a stable and progressive economic nation. Every leader's final obligation should be the preservation of the nation into one entity.

The Nigerian nation is going through series of crisis due to political bickering and less of compromise. Nigeria's unity is under heavy pressure. Every leader must know that to lead a divided nation into economic superpower position might lead to a risk of national survival itself.

The Nigerian nation today is faced with the most desparate emergencies. Nigeria's very survival is at stake and with it the very survival of the world's most populous black nation.

The military must know that it is not possible to lose the

nation and yet preserve the military. The military is nothing without the nation.

A President or Head-of-state is the representative and trustee of the Nigerian people. The national policy of Nigeria under any administration (be it military or civilian) should not be the personal perogative of the leader to decide without consultation from the people that are governed. A leader should be a shrewd and careful politician and must surround himself or herself with and listen to intelligent and strong people and must be sensitive to the voices of national and world opinion. Prudent leaders know that there is no policy that will succeed without popular support especially without the overwhelming support of the entire nation.

When economic affairs dominated the policy of a nation like Nigeria, its leaders must of necessity be its guide, must utter every judgement, must take every first step of action, must supply the information upon which it is to act to the people and must control its entire conduct. The President is the steward of the people and must conduct himself as such.

Most of the crisis that brew in Nigeria calls for flexibility of action because inflexible actions might drag the country into another civil war instead of keeping the country out of war. Nigerian leaders (both North and South) should sit down at a negotiating table and come up with compromises to avert a full-blown crisis; preventive diplomacy is the best remedy now, if not, when provocation becomes intolerable, there would be no remedy except a total war fought at a time when the country needs full-scale economic revolution.

A strong leader that believes in the unity of Nigeria and continued economic progress of the nation is one who acts with consultation and with notice. A leader's action will be right and legal if it could be shown that this action would

101

strengthen rather than weaken Nigeria's economic situation.

A good leader must be cautious, must be deeply sensitive to the ebb and flow of public opinion and must be aware that government is a process of consent and accountability.

The future of Nigeria now hangs in balance, the leadership is holding back instead of moving forward. The responsibility of any leader now is bringing a divided nation into the realm of economic reality. To do this, the leader must ensure that the country goes into economic progress as a united country.

The life of the nation is at stake and this brings justification for extreme measures. Like the civil war during General Yakubu Gowon's administration, the political crisis now has substantial public backing and the use of emergency power must be sustained. The Nigerian people want their government to act not merely to talk.

Nigeria's current obsession for a broad-based economic policy has brought a burdensome intrusion into the immediate concerns of Nigerians which is domestic affairs. There is distaste now in leadership almost amounting to horror for the chaotic disorder in the Nigerian political process.

The continued menace of unexpected crisis hangs over Nigeria and demands for the concentration within government for the means of instant decision and response.

Nigerians should be willing to be co-pilots in economic revolution take-offs as well as in the crash landings. Bi-partisanship should be the means to place national security above partisan advantage.

There are indispensable qualities that a leader must have,

and these are --- steadfastness in a cause, perseverance against difficulties, efficiency in the execution of policy, patience and prudence.

Every leader must act to preserve the safety of the nation. Every leader must save the nation from catastrophe. A leader's power has the advantage of concentration in one person who has been chosen by everybody and thus in consequence the focus of public hope and expectation. Nigerians of all ethnic groups need an alliance for progress.

The truth is that the military has been completely unable --- politically, technically and spiritually to give the Nigerian people the kind of leadership essential to the survival of the nation. The military has continued to accumulate power at the expense of the masses.

The June 12, 1993 annulment involved a wide range of reciprocal misperceptions as well as genuine differences in principle and clash of political interests. Each ethnic group confirmed the fears of the other and ultimately increased the interlocking illusion bred by crisis.

The Nigerian approach to domestic affairs, nourished in the sense of ever-present crisis, has set new political criteria and developed the military's ability for constant coup plotting. Armed intervention for political purposes obviously raises questions.

Nigerian Presidents should not mind disagreement. Disagreement should not bother any President. Unfortunately, disagreement bothers most Nigerian Presidents, especially, the military Head-of-state. They resist bad news, they are unwilling and never in touch with reality because they always clamor for conformity. They detest student uprising, protest in the press and on the street.

103

Nigeria has become a nation of decrees and laws, not a nation of human beings with compassion. The military has increased the problems of an already vaporous political society by making itself (the military) a small nation within a nation, united by their code of conduct, resentments of civilians, ambitions through coup plotting and possession of an enormous array of weapons. The military establishment, forgetting that when they retire, they no longer have all the paraphenellia that surrounds them when they are in active service, the military thus continue to destroy the civil and political rights of the Nigerian people.

Nigeria needs leaders that will use power to enlightened ends. The vast economic changes of the last decades have given new powers to leaders for increased usage of political consultations in government.

A leader must make it his or her duty to keep close to the people. The leader must be exposed to a wide range of national opinion. A strong leader must be strong with the people not strong against the people. Unfortunately, in the case of Nigeria most leaders are strong against the people. Isolation from the people and reality is definitely inseparable from the usage of power.

A leader must accept the obligation of accountability and the discipline of consent. A leader must incorporate within himself an array of diverse value from every ethnic group. A leader should see a greater variety of people, consult a wide range of opinion and tap more diversified sources of knowledge.

Most leaders in Nigeria unquestionably denied themselves of reality, especially when it comes to economic or political decisions. Most times reality forces them to hear and accept the unpleasant talk.

Most of the military leaders that the nation has been forced to witness has a belief that the nation was swarming with personal enemies, they detest face-to-face argument but prefer seclusion; and they have a penchant with response to crisis and a stubborn insistence on a controlled environment.

For the military leaders to succeed with the enormous power which they possess due to the huge arsenal they have, they need a succession of battles in a crisis-driven environment to be fought against their so-called enemies with every weapon available to their disposal.

A leader has to be a great interviewer to seek the truth and in this process must be patient in hearing the truth about the things he has inquired. In contrast, bad news is always an irritant to Nigerian leaders and anyone who is consistent with bearing bad news is ultimately exiled or secluded from the leaders' presence. Eventually, rather than hate the message, they hate the message bearer.

One of the most important means outside any administration to bring the leadership into reality is through the media of mass opinion --- newspapers, magazines and recently radio and television. Unfortunately for the country, 99.9% of the media establishments in the entire nation is set-up to benefit the political aims of the owners and their ethnic regions hence at every whim of dissent or misperception of what the administration sees as adverse publicity, the culprit media house is closed, there is no time for compromise, law suits or explanations.

If the media is to truly serve the federal republic of Nigeria in oneness, most leaders will discover that the press would be a forum in which they are not only told things but they learned things but in this sense how many Nigerian leaders are willing to learn? They believe that because they are in a position of leadership, that means learning has stopped. How many Nigerian leaders have you seen that choose reading as their past-time? If leaders are willing to learn, they should hold press-conferences often and preparation for the press-conferences requires the leader to acquaint himself or herself with matters of public scrutiny.

The questions asked at the conferences often discloses to the leader things about the administration and the country that his or her officials consciously or not had been keeping from the leader. The press conference should not be seen as a one-way street but a two-way forum of sharing of information.

For all its enormous vanities, ethnic bias and vagaries, the Nigerian press serves as the champion of reality against the leader for self-misconception. Meeting and fraternizing with the press will contribute immensely to the vitality and responsiveness of any leader and its administration. Instead Nigerian leaders detest the press and will only call on the press when they want something favorably disseminated. Any criticism is regarded as foul play. Forgetting that the only way to grow and progress is through constructive criticism. Any leader or any administration that feels it has been libeled can prosecute for seditious libel, that is why the courts are in existence but because these leaders do not respect the courts or are impatient leaders, the first thing that comes to their mind is the closure of media houses.

A very active press should be welcomed by a strong leader, even when you do not like when, what, why, how and where they disseminate stories. Although the press has not always (in any society, including the United Sates of America) discharge its duty with the utmost of intelligence and responsibility but one must be aware that the press is not a part of any administration hence has no reason or duty to support any administration.

Most military leaders regard the media and public debate in general without a disguised impatience and resentment. Some how, one can understand their behavior due to their way of operating. They are used to orders without questions hence they want the general public to behave the same way. Whatever is decreed by the military has to be swallowed wholeheartedly by the public without questions hence military leaders in their quest for power and supremacy are determined to put the media in their (so-called) place. The military can not, will not stand savage and unrelenting criticism from the media. They always see themselves as the pitiful and helpless victim of media conspiracy. They forget that open door policy with the media will not only serve the military to its advantage but will also serve the nation in proper and efficient way of dissemination of information. The military feels that open door policy with the media threatens to destroy all respect for established institutions.

The military has lost its value for war preparedness because each member of the military looks forward to political appointments instead of military assignments.

The military leaders have always assaulted the integrity of the media and called into question the media's right to disagree with official military views. The only way for administrations to succeed, is for Nigerian citizens and the media to speak their minds and consciences --- with-in the framework of the law and with a patriotic spirit. The military declines to listen to any form of criticism, they treat the media with studied contempt. This dislike of challenge and scrutiny from any quarters especially the media, explains the incessant closure of media houses.

The economic and political management of military administration is reputable incompetent. Not to discredit the military's quest for power, --- crisis and failure in political administration became the means of gaining power by the military . The politicians disadvantage became the military's advantage,

Most leaders in Nigeria use political power for economic ends. The essence of politics in a growing economy that is managed properly needs action.

Nigerians must realize that neither the Head-Of-State/President nor the Armed Forces Ruling Council (AFRC), Supreme Military Council/Executive Council of Ministers had the exclusive right to decide priorities unilaterally. By virtue of government, they are enjoined to make decisions together hence, from now on, when you want to point fingers at Generals Yakubu Gowon, Murtala Ramat Muhammed, Olusegun Obasanjo, Muhammadu Buhari, Ibrahim Badamasi Babangida and Sanni Abacha, or President Shehu Usman Aliyu Shagari, ---- I hope you will remember that in every decision that was carried out by each of these men in their administration, there was someone from your community that served with them, that also took part in the decision making process and the final decision itself. So if you must blame these men for any misdeeds, you must also call to question the person from your community that served with these men; did they serve your community, did they serve the nation or did they serve their own selfish interest to the best of their ability. Although, the bucks stops with the Head-Of-State or President but accountability and responsibility should be shared by everyone including advisers.

With each military coup, the same revolution emerged, the essence of this revolution is not power to the people but

108

instead it is power to the Head-Of-State/Presidency.

The military in essence, has not stolen power, instead, politicians had surrendered power out of fear of responsibility and recognition of incapacity. Politicians are even without pride and they usually wait humbly by the military and licked the hands of their oppressors.

Everyone agrees with the diagnosis that the country's economy is in a mess but no one seems to come up or agree with a prescription. For any leader to succeed today, he or she must invent programs for war against poverty.

In politics as in real life, you win some you lose some but in Nigerian politics you have to win it all or lose it all. Most military leaders, instead of conciliating the minority ethnic groups, they are always cold and unforgiving to the minority. Instead of placating the minority, they confront them with all sorts of decrees.

The military has a climate of excessive concern over the political impact of student or public demonstrations. They regard riots, burning of properties as one of the dangers to the federal government.

Any person or group of persons that are perceived to be in opposition of the ruling administration is dealt with by using any available federal machinery. They believe that student unrest is the product of political agitators and subversive elements from the South, who are out to discredit any military regime regardless of the regime's agenda. They refuse to believe that political activists or student militants are acting on their own. They insist that they are one and the same people and that all their activities are sponsored or financed by politicians from the South. On the basis of personal theories of national security, theories that were not explained to the people but aimed at Southerners, the military in a bid to continue its grip on power, constantly threatens the Nigerian people with incarcerations.

Nigeria has a situation where public officials do things for their own private advantage. They have a conduct of public affairs for private gain. They have always believed that stealing public money for oneself is an old Nigerian tradition that is here to stay. So far, Nigerians have not found angels in the form of public servants to govern them.

The Head-of-state or President represents the whole people of the federal republic of Nigeria, while each member of the Armed Forces Ruling Council/Supreme Military Council or Executive Council of Ministers only represents portions of their states of origin. The decisions reached or ratified by the SMC, AFRC, or Executive Council of Ministers does not necessarily mean that it represents the majority of the people of Nigeria or reflects the true will of the Nigerian people.

To deplete the authority of the military and to stop the proliferation of coups, people have suggested that resources of the military establishment should be slashed so that it will not be attractive to join the military except in time of war.

The Nigerian people do not know exactly how much money the military establishment spends each year on intelligence nor do they have any idea what the military intelligence actually does with the money. Is military intelligence to help the nation against aggression from outside or to crack down on opposition to the ruling military administration in the nation? Common sense will tell you that it should be intelligence about other countries, instead most of the intelligence operations is based on inflicting excruciating pain on the average Nigerian citizen. All the intelligence services in the country should concentrate on intelligence collection and analysis.

A leader must have insight, character, devotion and modesty so as to bring warring factions into common grounds of counsel. The truly strong leader is not the one who relies on his power to command, the truly strong leader is the one who recognizes his responsibility and accountability and knows that as a leader he or she has the opportunity to enlighten and persuade the people. Most leaders in Southern Nigeria tend to be lone-rangers concerned and pre-occupied with shorting-up individual power base and creating individual reputations instead of community power and community reputations.

Southerners resentment over exclusion of Presidential power has become unbearable and it has led to series of crisis, riots, labor unrest and political querells. Inherent traditional devices could make a contribution to the task of accommodating each other. But these traditional values will not work unless there is a will on both sides (i.e. North and South) to make them work. The Northerners must have the will and urge to share and Southerners must also have the will to take responsibility and stop personal jealousies. One of the major problems of Southerners is not the lack of power but the lack of courage to use the educational power they posses. The Nigerian Presidential power should reside in joint possession between the North and the South not just soley in the hands of the Northerners.

Every responsible journalist in Nigeria must ask themselves these pertinent questions before doing a story -- Is it news? Is it in the interest of the nation's security? Most humiliations Nigerians receive abroad is due to news stories they claim to have read in Nigerian dailies that are unpatriotic and degrading. Editors and publishers should know that the decision to publish news affecting national security must be based on a grander standard and that of just news judgement.

We should stop talking about the future, we should do something about the future now, we should create solutions for the existing problems now. We should now have an era of negotiation instead of an era of continuous confrontation.

The military governments has always rejected openness, candor and mutual respect for civilians, instead they favored insolent and sycophancy, forgetting that any government that is run by duplicity, lies and crisis-domination is doomed for failure.

Nigerians must be efficiently informed about past administrations so that future administrations will improve and correct the mistakes of the past. Ultimately, knowledge of the past means an acceptance of responsibility for the future -- knowledge is a potent medicine.

Military administrations are created by crisis at home in a bold bid for political power at home. Most leaders (both military and politicians) have not risen to the ethical standard of the position of Presidency or Head-of-state. Most have been unfaithful to the trust of the office, most have soiled the name of the nation. The Nigerian nation and her citizens have a clear right to expect that they will always have wise and righteous leaders who are willing to stand by the principles of the law and be compassionate, instead the nation and its citizens have witnessed an array of ambitious men, who seek power for their own self-interests with absolute despicable hatred for liberty and a great contempt for the law, but have a love affair with crisis so as to stay in power.

Nigeria is a nation blessed with enormous human resources, it is also richly endowed with natural resources --

oil, iron, and steel, gold etc. but unfortunately , the nation is retrogressing instead of progressing, due to large-scale corruption and political turmoil.

In good times, an appointment to cabinet level position is the highest responsibility any one could expect and it calls for the grandest of conduct. Today, most people looked back to the administration they serve with shame and horror.

A leader should devote himself or herself entirely to the problem of the Nigerian nation and free himself or herself from partisan politics, because sycophants can give you everything you want --- food, drink, helicopters, girlfriends, boyfriends, etc. but they will not give you relief from political problems.

Leaders should be set free from ethnic politics and allowed to do what is best for the country. The people most of the time, knows what the leaders do not know and already the people pay a huge price for the leaders isolation and ignorance. Leaders must concern themselves with public opinions instead of worries about their own political future. Leaders must extend power to the Nigerian people instead of locking the people hand and foot by rigid decrees.

Every administration in order to succeed and for posterity (either military or politician) must accept a full sense of responsibility to explain itself in every action or policy to the Nigerian people.

We are in an era when political turbulence, ethnicity, poverty, sky-high inflation, crime (acute armed-robbery) and self-interest is straining the fragile bond of national cohesion and the spirit of togetherness. Nigeria needs strong leaders that will hold the nation together.

The only effective means of correcting injustice in the nation is to be fair. We need the watchful interference of the press and the people and the resolute interference of a responsible government to effect fair play in justice. It is only able leadership that will take Nigeria into the next century.

In every action taken by leaders of any administration, it must be accompanied by clear public explanation and tested by public acceptance. A strong leader must be sensitive to the diversity of concerns and opinions of the Nigerian people. A strong leader must maintain divergent range of contacts and surround himself or herself with the most articulate and positive thinking advisers and use them to clarify issues and try out people and policies for the ruling administration. Everyday, we learn, not through abstractions but we learn, through real people and through real situations.

Nigerians should be able to resolve their differences without bloodshed or imprisonment. Everything that has been achieved in the United States or anywhere in the world has always been through individual effort, even when it is a government achievement, it was dreamed or convened by an individual before it became a government achievement, hence I implore every Nigerian to stop criticizing the government, start to give back to your country by dreaming big and pursuing your dreams into reality.

Corruption, increase crime wave and a devastating high unemployment have eroded the wealth, values and cultural standards of the country. Freedom is not free anywhere in the world, you must pay a price for freedom, freedom and its price should entail one for all, all for one.

We have too many leaders in the South clamoring for every available political position but getting these leaders to work together to achieve the goals of the Nigerian people is the major problem of the nation. Most leaders in the North and in the South, share a believe that compromise shows feebleness, hence, instead of compromise, they go into the extreme method of winner takes all.

Leaders in the South or North, must make a difference, think positive, before you take a step forward you have to take a step backward because, if you forget where you come from you will not know where you are going ---- so educate to elevate. Leaders must know that equal opportunity with government assistance is a moral thing to do. Both military and political leaders should know that, out of honest differences of opinion comes solutions for Nigeria's problems.

A free and responsible media is very essential in the country, a free media will expose falsehood and hypocrisy wherever it exists. Every government official should know that information is a weapon ----- a very important weapon that must be used to educate the people of Nigeria.

The media in Nigeria is accepted as the fourth estate or to put it bluntly the fourth branch of government (i.e. after the executive, the house of assembly or the supreme military council/armed forces ruling council and the judiciary). The media has always served as the people's watchdog over government and government activities.

The goal of the media has always been to take the position of the ordinary citizen who is not able to be present at government activities and government policies. The Nigerian media in essence has and should always be the ears and the eyes of the ordinary citizen.

The role of the media is that of making the government ---- the peoples government. If the media does not probe the government constantly in a responsible manner, the Nigerian people will remain uninformed and ultimately, there will be a vacuum between the government and those governed.

The media must operate an independent stand-point from the government; Radio, Television, Magazines and Newspapers must narrate to the people of Nigeria the element of government's policies and objectives. The media and the government are the two arms that almost always depend on each other. Both the media and the government are powerful institutions but their power must not be to the detriment of the people, instead their power should enhance the people in their day-to-day activities.

The government and the media always clash because both institutions have different objectives. The media increasingly tries to get and report the truth, while on the other arm, the government tries to present its policies and objectives in a favorable manner. Hence, while the media tries to report the facts without undue partisanship, the government tries to paint its activities to its advantage, thus bringing a collusion course between the government and the media. Direct access to information about the government is essential for the media to work effectively.

For the country to maintain an administration (military or civilian) to function properly, the people must be informed accurately. Every government leader must have the confidence of representing the people of the nation and one of the ways to have that confidence is for the government official and the government itself to acknowledge that the people are well-informed.

The media and the people have the innate right to criticize the decisions of the government responsibly. The leader of the government and his or her cabinet must have credibility in order to function successfully.

Every leader should cultivate a personal relationship with news correspondents. A leader must always be in touch with the people and the media. Leaders must acknowledge the simple fact that the news media can not be partners with the government in determining what is newsworthy, the government and the news media must work in cohesion but in separate ways. The news media can not afford any censorship in order to protect the government (military or civilian)against criticism. The government also can not afford not to listen to the media and public opinion. The government should not regard the media as a conduit to be used only when they want to relay self-serving information about the government. The public needs to be educated with the truth and clear facts not despicable propaganda. Effective news management as a principle is very good.

A leader of the government must be a master politician, an accomplished leader, a leader that will be able to manage and share power with the people. A leader should have the ability to serve as an effective shaper of public opinion. Before and after a government policy is enacted, the public and the government must have debates of alternatives in the national interest.

Most leaders know that information is power and power is wealth and they are not ready to share this wealth, that is why they keep most information to themselves. Leaders must not intimidate the media or else face alienation by the media. Most leaders are sensitive about what is written or spoken about them in the media, they only prefer what is favorable to them. A leader will always lose in any confrontations with the media.

Amongst the horrendous legacies that bad leaders

117

(military or civilian) have left in the nation are huge mismanagement of the economy, in-humane policies and mass corruption.

Every President or Head-of-state that has been at the helm of affairs of the nation had to appeal to Southerners as an economizer ---- one who appreciates money and knows how to spend it on priorities, while he or she must appeal to the Northerners as a sympathetic spender ------ one who gives them any booty they want and increase the defense budget spending, to the advantage of the Northerners.

PAST POLITICAL LEADERS

Past leaders have destroyed the country politically and economically. Some of the ways that led to the colossal waste of human and natural resources include but not limited to ---- - 1. waste of public money, 2. lack of accountability and 3. sinking enormous proportion of money on projects which were in truth conduits for siphoning public funds into private bank accounts.

Leaders in Nigeria must end the rulership of the country by one ethnic group, one religious group, one region and rulership of self-interest.

Most leaders think, if you are not one of Nigeria's fittest, you may not be one of Nigeria's finest. Leaders must know that bad policies today are tomorrow's consequences.

Past political parties were not national parties, they were all based on tribe and ethnic groups and sometimes regional and religious affiliations.

Some military officers in the country now prefer political appointments over regimental appointments. The Nigerian State Security Service (SSS) should not be involved in the torture and killing of Nigerian citizens.

The political elite in Nigeria must be compassionate, matured, consistent, patriotic, considerate, compromising, principled, resolute, purposeful, selfless and most of all visionary.

Nigeria is witnessing omens of destruction everywhere in the country, people now grasp at solutions offered by a guilt culture; more police, more lawyers, more courts, more prisons, more litigation, more regulations and more death squads.

Right now, Nigeria instead of being led by a shame culture that educates by persuasion, by showing the right thing to do, is now unfortunately having the guilt culture that educates by fear of the consequences of doing the wrong thing.

Leadership must prepare Nigerians for the coming century. Leaders have to do it through education and compassion. Leaders must teach Nigerians the unquestioning faith in the power of education.

The economy of Nigeria is a resource economy. And one would assume that wherever the most highly needed natural resources were to be found, employment opportunities would follow, but not so in Nigeria. All the natural resources are found in the rural areas of the country but all the employment opportunities are based in the cities -- especially in Lagos, Abuja, Kaduna and Kano.

In contrast, the most rapidly growing industries of the 1990's in the developed world are: microelectronics, biotech, the new material-science industries, telecommunications, civilian aircraft manufacturing, machine tools and robots, and computers --- these are all brainpower industries that could be located anywhere in the world. Where these industries will take root and flourish depends upon who organizes the brainpower to acquire them. And who organizes the power most efficiently will depend on who educates toward that objective best.

Product invention, if one is also not the world's low-cost producer, gives a country very little economic advantage. Being the low-cost producer is partly a matter of wages, but to a much larger extent it is a matter of having the skills necessary to put new things together. Wages do not depend on an individual's skill and productivity alone. To a large extent they reflect team skills and team productivities.

The value of any single person's knowledge depends upon the smartness with which that knowledge is used in the entire economic system i.e. the abilities of buyers and supplies to absorb that individual's skills.

Every economy is a dynamic economy and always in transition. Most companies that perform best are those that are able to move from one product to another product within the technological families very fast that they can always keep one generation ahead. If Nigeria wants to stay ahead at the leading edge of technology and continue to generate high wages and profits, Nigeria must be a participant in the evolutionary progress of brainpower industries so as to be in a position to take proper advantage of the technical and economic revolutions that normally arise. Knowledge has become the major source of long-run sustainable competitive advantage.

Studies have continued to show that rates of return for industries and countries that invest in knowledge and skills are more than double those of industries and countries that concentrate only on plant and equipment. Also, the countries that offer companies the lowest costs of developing technological leadership will be the countries that invest the most in research and development, education and infrastructure.

The skill sets required in the economy of the future will be radically different from those required today and in the past. The implications for the future are profoundly simple. If Nigeria wants to generate a high standard of living for all its citizens, skill and knowledge development are crucial.

New brainpower industries must be invented and acquired. Organizing brainpower means not just building a research and development system that will put Nigeria on the leading edge of technology, but organizing a top-to-bottom work force that has the brainpower necessary to make Nigerians masters of the new production and distribution technologies that will allow Nigeria to be the world's low-cost producers. To do all these will require a very different Nigerian educational system and leadership. Building such a system and leadership is the ultimate new Nigerian challenge.

The people of Nigeria are looking for leaders who have proven the ability to successfully transfer their knowledge and skills to a variety of functions or organizations. Money, status and opportunity continues to divide Nigerians. The social problems are rooted in hate, greed and a maldistribution of wealth.

Drugs, violence and crime are the consequence of poverty, ignorance and despair. The poor in the country lies in appalling conditions, huddled together in squalid tenements. They suffer mightily from crime, illegitimacy, substance abuse and violence. These problems are brought on by deprivation and injustice.

What the 90's and beyond are calling for are "multi specialists" -- i.e. leaders who know more than one area in depth. These are the leaders that will have an edge in today and tomorrow's economic/political leadership.

Nigeria needs "multi-capable" leaders to handle multiple responsibilities. What matters today and in the future is results. It is not enough for leaders to simply have held certain positions and responsibilities, the people want to know --- what have you done with positions and responsibilities you have had? What have you accomplished while in a given leadership role? Have you met or exceeded the people's goals? Leaders must be able to point to specific accomplishments. Also leaders must give themselves an advantage in today's leadership environment by changing their leadership style. Leaders today must make the shift from being an approver or dictator to being a coach or mentor.

Leadership and the people of Nigeria must shift emphasis from the public sector to the private sector so as to turn the economy around into prosperity. Private companies should work diligently to diversify their client bases. Most of them that started out primarily focused on federal government contracting should develop not only commercial clients for their products and services, but opportunities with foreign governments and foreign companies. The private sector must increase the nature of the economy. High technology is the key driver of the private sector and the national economy.

Today's leaders must understand that they have to acquire new knowledge because new technologies are wiping out old knowledge and old skills. People generally study to stay current, but they also want something extra, they want new knowledge that will make them attractive to their current and or prospective employers. People know and feel that acquiring new knowledge is insurance to their own future.

Leadership must make the Nigerian people recognize the importance of creating wealth individually i.e. through private enterprises. The individual's interest in collective cultures lies not just in rituals, customs, identity or artistic accomplishment. Instead the individual's interest must be on the fundamental aspects of culture that yield living standard advances based on material development.

What is most crucial about cultures is that they develop a role of an enormous accumulations of human capital in a structured way.

Human capital should be more than education, expertise or skill; human capital is a set of attitudes and values. It is not the specific skills brought from Igbo land which produces the greatest economic success for the Igbos, but it is their more general human capital in work/business habits, perseverance, social and community cohesion. The Igbos are not too proud to wear rags and to do the hardest and dirtiest work rejected by other tribes. Although with all these attributes to the Igbos, there is still the inevitability of unequal outcomes; because, due to competition, people are ultimately distributed in the social order according to their particular abilities to produce and acquire wealth.

The people of Nigeria need a decisive leader, a leader who is broad-based, a leader who is sensitive to various personal and human issues involved in rescuing a troubled nation. A leader who has analytical skills, an understanding of financial data and the courage to take corrective action with compassion. This leader must also have the ability to motivate the people and build consensus, also the leader must have the willingness to listen to the people.

A leader must have the trait of an inherent ability to lead diverse ethnic groups of people, motivate them, put them together as a team and to get them to do and accomplish things they may believe are beyond their capability.

One of the most important news coming from the United States of America that some of the Nigerian people are yet to comprehend is that among the notable changes of the last decades has been the shift from large companies to smaller companies as the primary contributors to new job growth in the United States. Of every three new jobs created in the last decade, two of them have been with companies under one hundred (100) employees.

In predicting more of the same trend for the foreseeable future, research indicates by the year 2000 and beyond, eighty (80) percent of workers in the United States of America will work with firms of less than 200 employees.

Nigeria and Nigerians should take note and stop waiting for the federal, state and local governments for job creation and accumulation of wealth; the country needs private and individual investors in business to create jobs and security for the people of Nigeria and the future of Nigeria.

Nigeria, Africa's cornerstone --- powerful, populous and oil-rich must produce immediately leadership with compassion. Due to bad leadership of the past, the economy of the country dissolved, federal, state and local government employees went months without pay. Educational standards crumbled, teachers went months without pay.

Ethnicity must not be manipulated in the Nigerian society. People may be from the North or the South, but in the end they should realize that they belong to ONE nation and that is the federal entity called Nigeria.

Strong leadership is needed that will take steps to reduce the military influence without the risk of provoking a coup. The leader must confront the military without publicly humiliating the military. Part of the evolution toward a civil society for Nigeria is for the military and the civilians to engage in talks that will foster mutual understandings and compromise for the benefit of Nigeria and Nigerians.

The military, while insisting that no weak nation can move forward, must also come to the grim conclusion that they must adapt or die --- there is no other choice. Every military person was a civilian before entering the military and will remain a civilian after leaving the military.

Regardless of who rules Nigeria (military or civilian), the major problems that needs to be solved by good and strong leadership are: 1. enough food for the masses and some for export, 2. clean water, 3. efficient and reliable electricity, 4. good roads, 5. reduction of unemployment , 6. decrease in crime, 7. efficient and reliable public transportation network throughout the federation, 8. good communication network, 9. adequate housing and 10. self-less leaders that believes in job performance and accountability.

Leaders in Nigeria, need to realize that in order to fulfill the hopes and aspirations of the citizens, leadership demands, grace, candor and honesty. Leaders must lead a crucial war against poverty and hunger. Policies must be put in place to assist the vast numbers of disadvantage citizens.

The nation and her citizens must look to the future with enormous emphasis on avoiding the encore of past mistakes by irresponsible leadership. The nation needs leaders with administrative skills, dreamers, doers, intelligent and an ultimate huge desire to improve the living standards of the people of Nigeria.

Nigeria does not need any leader that is a divider, a schemer and a destroyer. The nation needs a leader who can build.

The people of Nigeria blame government and its leaders for everything but what about leaders in the business sectors, there is no law that says, it is only government that must do everything. The business sector reports billions of Naira in profits every year in Nigeria, what are they doing with all that profit, how many percentage of these profits have they given back to the country to improve the living standards of the Nigerian people. Which of the leaders of any big company has made sure that out of its profits some funds must go back to the community through building of roads, clean water, agriculture, adequate housing, loans, community-based employment, expansion into rural areas, science projects, research, electricity, etc. Unless these huge conglomerates assist the leaders of Nigeria, the leader is destined for failure because for a leader to succeed, there must be economic backing from the business sector.

Corruption is so widespread in the political and military institutions that it has undermined the political/military relationship with the people of Nigeria. Most leader's concerns in the country is political not humanitarian.

You must be a devout nationalist to rule Nigeria. You can not be a sectional leader and say you are a true leader. Of all the leaders Nigeria has had till date, many people believe that the only true national leader the country ever had is General Yakubu Gowon --- may be this was due to his young age, he was able to see beyond regional politics, ethnic groups and religious bickering.

Every other leader before and after General Yakubu Gowon, regardless of the pretense, has always and will continue to be either regional, ethnic, religious or sectional leaders, non of them was in the true sense national leaders, they may pretend to be federalists but only to the advantage of their region, ethnic, religious or sectional area.

When General Ibrahim Badamasi Babangida was spending all those billions of Naira on political transition

128

programs, how many Nigerian leaders in and out of his cabinet, called him privately and publicly to alert him that political transition does not need billions of Naria, instead, just hand-over power to a civilian elected President and use the political transition billions of Naira for immediate necessities such as adequate food, good roads, adequate housing, reduction of unemployment, reduction of crime etc.

No responsible leader should pursue political transition and abandon all other aspects of national existence. People criticize the economy of Nigeria but how many people actually contribute to making the economy better. The culture, values and the economy are all geared toward the pursuit of ultimate and absolute power by the political elite and the military. The Igbos are the only ethnic group that have businesses throughout the entire federation and thus contribute immensely to the economy of Nigeria.

A leader should be able to take the initiative in influencing public-opinion, project ideas from various quarters and seek public support for government policies. Every leader has a responsibility to keep the public informed, to ensure accountability. Enlightening the public's mind is a must by the government and its leader.

A strong and compassionate leader is the one that holds the key to Nigeria's future. The nation needs to invest more on scientific research programs and give scientists all the encouragement and finance they need because the ultimate goal of any science program is the excellence of human life with inventions and wealth. Science also helps to improve the quality of life for Nigerians.

Everything Nigerian scientists attempt must be empowered with success. Nigerian scientists must be encouraged to test the foreground of new, old and existing technology.

Nigeria needs NEW LEADERSHIP and closer attention from the people and intrinsic improvements in the NEW LEADERSHIP attitude towards the need to inform the people sincerely.

The military's annual budget has always been more than half of the total budget of Nigeria, hence, they derive their perplexing power from two major sources --- 1. money and 2. the huge arsenal of weapons that only money can buy. The huge size and the intricacy of the military constantly threatens the people to be fully informed of the activities of the military. The military can not be seen as too complicated for public scrutiny.

Leaders must not be seen as encouraging crisis instead of talking peace. If there is crisis in any administration (military or civilian) it is not a crisis of compromise but a crisis of confidence between the leaders and the people.

A leader, though wise, can not be wiser than the entire people. It is the people that must decide what is good for them not the government, the government has no choice but to listen to the aspirations of the people. A leader and the government must find out what the people want and give the people what they want, that is the ultimate challenge of any leader or any government but in the case of Nigeria, the leader and the government gives the people what the leader and the government want, hence the proliferation of leaders and governments.

Every administration should insist on the dissemination of thoughts from different sources to ensure the well-being of the Nigerian people. The government, at all times must be dependent on the free flow of ideas from different sources.

True opinion is very essential for honest governance. True opinions lead to consensus with the leader and the people.

For most Nigerian leaders it has been very easy to manipulate the people than to persuade them, it has been easier for the leaders to submerge the media with statements, propaganda and private interviews to the people. The media has always been condemned by each administration for criticism it has made. Leaders must know that in order for people to perform effectively as citizens they must have access to the truth about government affairs. The entire foundation of government should be based on truth. Leaders in Nigeria have to realize that in every government, "soja go soja come" but the only boss in Nigeria is the Nigerian people. The people of Nigeria are the master, every leader is a servant of the people and the only way for a leader to be good is to serve the will of the people. The only way for the leader to be successful is to let the master of the society ----- the people rule the society.

Strong leadership is required to bring order out in every chaos that the country experiences. The people are the ones that have the right to supervise the government. Every administration must encourage the participation of every citizen in government. Every administration must ensure the people's right to know the affairs of government. Every leader must have the interest of the people and ensure the people's right to know the affairs of government. Nigerian leaders (both South and North) must and should realize that cooperation and compromise is a two-way street. New leaders should be more suited to the national interest of the nation than sectional or ethnic prejudice and with strong and dedicated leadership the country will move forward to the future, stronger and more prosperous.

The Nigerian media (regardless of fear or threat of

131

imprisonment) should be less inclined with preserving the military or political elite and should be more concerned with admonishing the leadership and exposing them when they are not doing the right thing. The Nigerian people are the strength of the nation, the Nigerian people are the only ones who know how to solve their problems. Improvement of the welfare of the Nigerian people requires strong and compassionate leadership.

Nigerians, collectively and individually both in Nigeria and outside the country must safeguard the future of the nation today not tomorrow. Nigerians are looking for heroes, a hero that will be known for achievements, someone that will show Nigerians the possibilities of human nature and to make history. Nigerians are very capable of things that have not been revealed yet.

Most military leaders sacrifice human lives for loyalty. Political parties in the South are always riddled with sabotage and innate struggle for power.

All the non-oil producing states must find out a way to generate money instead of depending on the federation account from the federal government for in-frequent hand-outs.

To be able to accomplish any goals, Nigerians must be willing to work hard and they must have people who believe in them. People can only be strong when they work together. People must also be willing to sacrifice ----- materially, physically and emotionally for their believes and must ensure that they give back to their community.

Every leader should be concerned about their environment, the community, the poor, the uneducated and the less-privileged.

Quality leadership should and must be held in high esteem than achievement based on corruption and mismanagement. The leaders of the nation are responsible for ensuring that Nigerians are adequately equipped to compete in the global economy of the 21st century. The nation can not get any problems solved without the inconvenience of people, hence Nigerians must take responsibility for the past, present and the future, the ultimate rewards for such actions for both Nigeria and Nigerians are enormous. Most Nigerians seem to depend on politicians, educators, business leaders and military administrators to solve the nation's social and economic problems without realizing that the solutions to every problem lies with every individual.

Unless the people of Nigeria are intensely involved in every aspect of the political process, the government ultimately will collapse because any government that does not take the people's participation into consideration is a government that is not for the people.

Consumers in Nigeria are paying more for products and services and they are getting less in return, while industries and banks are reporting huge profits.

In the search for truth, the Nigerian media must not and can not be intimidated by power, either political power or military power.

People never want to identify with failure, everybody wants to identify with a winner, yet most of the military and political personnel of past failed leadership continue to participate in present administrations and Nigerians either look the other way or they encourage and prod these failed leaders to continue to occupy leadership positions.

The radical conservatives in the South and in the North

has no agenda, only hatred. Nigerians should look forward to the day when the entire country will be tribe-blind, when everyone regardless of tribe, ethnic, religion and creed will have common-purpose in the political and social process of the nation. This common-purpose of oneness is the only thread that will bind a fragmented nation such as Nigeria together. Let us put aside the things that divide us and come together as a unit and bring the issues that unite us. Dissenting the Northernization or islamitization or Southenization or Christianization of Nigeria is a political goal that Northerners and Southerners must be able to agree upon.

Most of the balk of money in Nigeria's treasury comes from oil sales at the Nigerian National Petroleum Corporation (N.N.P.C.) and instead of giving developments to the communities where the oil sales accrue, the money is being spent in development projects in Ajaokuta Steel Complex and other grandiose projects in states that are not oil producing states. Oil money is being used by the federal government to rescue states that do not produce oil from economic disaster. The proliferation of state creation did not consider how these states were going to create income-earning industries in these states. I can not in any rational sense understand how any government can create a state without any single visible industry in any part of that state. Most of the states in the federation depend solely on their income from the federal government's federation accounts. It makes you wonder why these non-industrial states were created in the first place, but wonder no more because they were created due to political considerations not economic viability. The oil companies in the nation and other multinational concerns have no major long-term investments in the communities where they make their horrendous profits. Most of the new states are civil service oriented and they depend hugely on the federal government.

The newly created states, instead of them to learn from the past mistakes of the old states, these new states also plunged into financial disaster through mismanagement, misplacement of priorities and most of all official corruption.

The country has a company owned by the federal government ----- the Nigerian Security Printing and Minting Company (N.S.P.M.C.), which amongst other responsibilities is responsible for printing bank notes, yet the government in 1993, awarded contracts to De La Rue Company Limited, a British Security Printing Company for the printing of billions of bank notes and you wonder why there are fake bank notes in the country.

Politicians and military officials are always blocking plans to start work on any project that is not an advantage to the person, regardless, if this project is of advantage to the people of the state and the country in general --- e.g. metro rail, rehabilitation of NITEL building, Independence building etc.

The other aspects of corruption, mismanagement and misappropriation is that of university Dons that were cabinet ministers in political and military administrations, one would think and conclude that these intellectuals would lead good example instead they are susceptible to massive mismanagement, misplacement of priorities and corruption in public office. These university Dons who prior to being appointed as cabinet ministers or into high public office, always criticize government officials but as soon as they mount the chairs of any high public office, the first and foremost thing they do is indulge themselves in a spending drift of personal comfort and self-enrichment.

Bringing sanity and prudence on the economic and political affairs of the nation deserves strong and compassionate leadership. The nation and its leaders must strive for sustainable economic and political growth. The economic and political problems in Nigeria stems from among other things ---- civil strife, poor or extremely bad leadership and the will of not being able to compromise on issues as well as political office. Political stability merged with economic market reforms in Nigeria would bring massive foreign investors to the country by industrialists that are attracted by a cheap labor force.

Every leader in the country should ascertain and reenforce the notion to every citizen in the country that agriculture still holds the key to Nigeria's economic solutions. Agricultural production on a massive scale is still the only key that is needed in Nigeria to generate income, to improve food security, help improve malnutrition and above all eliminate poverty in the entire society of Nigeria. Public and private investment programs must be encouraged on a high scale.

So far, what the Nigerian populace is witnessing is that, the military elite and the old brigade politicians are incapable of representing the grassroots because they are all stained by their cashroots in which they are committed to their military colleagues and the political elites. With this in mind, Nigerians have concluded that unless there is effective change in leadership, the people say they will continue to expect what they have always gotten ----- more corrupt public officials that do not care about the people but only care about their selfish pockets. The cynicism about government has not been dispelled by the military administrations nor political administrations, instead it has increased the people's cynicism towards government.

Most politicians and military personnel did not get what the June 12th proponents revulsion was; this was a genuine people's anger and pent-up frustration from a 30 years plus

136

build-up of rage. Such rage cannot be overcome by simple military decrees, these rage can only be overcome by reason and compassionate leadership that must realize that the most compelling evidence is the continued leadership of the Northerners in the high office of the Presidency or Head-of-state.

It is fascinating to know that, it is only in Nigeria and sub-saharan Africa, that leaders will have so much and the people have nothing. The leaders pride themselves for having so much and pretend not to see the excruciating pain that the poor masses are experiencing, people can not even afford one square meal a day, yet some leaders are seen washing their hands with bottles of expensive champagne at night parties instead of water.

Nigerians should not abdicate their burden of individual responsibility for a continued dependence on government. Government can not and must not continue to be responsible for everything, people must be personally responsible for some things. To be a good Nigerian citizen, people must be responsible both for their communities and themselves. People should stop blaming the government for everything, Nigerian citizens all over the world and especially those in the country should start asking themselves ----- what can I do to solve Nigeria's problems now? Not later. Until we arrive at a positive conclusion of what solutions to bring to our great and blessed nation, Nigerian people will continue to be their own worst enemy.

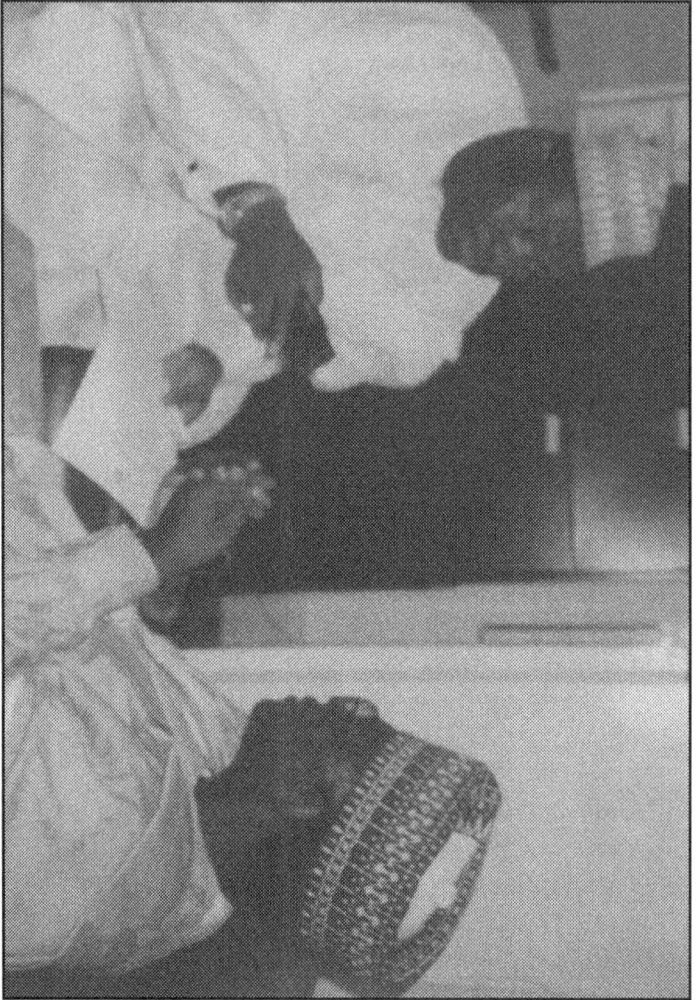

TONY OYATEDOR IN AN INTERVIEW WITH NIGERIA'S AMBASSADOR
TO THE UNITED STATES OF AMERICA, ALHAJI KAZAURE

NEW LEADERSHIP

The leaders of both military and civilian administrations have been embroiled in massive corruption and personal enrichment on a spectacular scale at the expense of the Nigerian people and most of all indifference to the physical and social deterioration of a nation that is a very blessed country.

The new leadership in Nigeria should be empowered by Nigerians eager for a full share of prosperity. The people that are united will never be defeated. We can not glorify the past administrations by continued re-appointment of those who participated in all the failed administrations without retrogression. Political participation without Southern representation in the office of the Presidency is infinitely wrong. Nigerians regardless of ethnic background must pledge to work together as one team to solve Nigeria's economic, social and political problems. We must get ready for tomorrow today.

Times have changed and Nigeria must change with the times to look its future with prosperity. Diversity is one of the keys for economic survival in Nigeria. Another thing that will contribute greatly in the economic survival of Nigeria is value of human life. The government must spend more money on public safety. Most money bags in communities, build nice, huge, beautiful homes and nothing else to offer the communities, no industries, no recreation centers, absolutely nothing else.

The economic reforms in the country, that was initiated entirely by the military has no connection to the root concerns of the people. The people of Nigeria do not know whom to trust when it comes to economic reforms. They do not trust the politicians neither do they trust the military. The government (military or civilians) do not have any survey data to understand the priorities of the people of Nigeria, the only data in the nation has been government priorities that are forced on the people. If the government ever attempt to do a survey and ask Nigerians what issues concerns them most, they will find out that the responds will not state that among the two or three biggest problems facing the country are government leadership in civilian clothes or military uniform, instead respondents will tell you that their biggest concerns are hunger, unemployment, adequate housing, efficient electricity, low inflation and most of all good and self-less leadership.

The ebullient trend-watchers are either ignoring or missing the treacherous upswing of the poor masses in Nigeria. The downtrodden poor masses amidst the country that is blessed with wealth is now threatening the foundations of Nigerian society. The poor masses are alienated from the political process and economic prosperity, hence their ultimate disposition toward crime. The government must interpose on behalf of the poor masses. Leaders must commit themselves to the upliftment of the poor masses.

The poor masses can not afford to travel overseas on exile when things are not going on fine at the home-front, they are too poor to buy or build beautiful houses, too poor to afford three-square meals, instead they quietly stay hungry.

Despite the wide-spread poverty and long suffering that this affronts breed, these poor masses have remained silent but not for long, because if the government does not step-in to invest on the poor people, these poor masses will soon explode.

The abandonment of the poor by the government must

discontinue and the people must be given a voice in government policy. The people's need must be taken care of first before the needs of the political elite. The indignation the poor people feel towards the wealthy-class often leads the poor into permanent life of crime. My hope and prayer is that the poor's anger and frustration should not be allowed to persevere because if it continues it could bring a trend of violence that will inflict excruciating pain in the entire country.

This imminent devastation must be stopped. Fundamental issues that is of paramount concern to the people must be addressed on a long-term basis. Be rest assured, I am not advocating the re-distribution of the money from wealthy Nigerians to the poor Nigerians, instead I am advocating that the wealthy Nigerians start to be compassionate so as to help the poor get out of poverty.

The leaders must remember that there are lessons to be learnt in a nation's economic failures and successes and these lessons must supply credible discernment to future leadership of the country.

If Nigeria will succeed in her quest for economic recovery and economic prosperity, government and the people must insist on placing able, strong and responsible leaders in leadership positions, leaders must ask for support from the people and from all politicians regardless of what party is in power. A concerted effort must be made to win public support for any economic or political policy.

Most of the key factors that contribute to the economic doldrums of the nation are -- mass corruption by public officials, excessive public spending without priorities, lack of investment in/by the private sector, tribalism and most of all bad political and military leadership without directions,

141

leaders that did not know if they were going or coming.

Fundamentally, the country needs a common objective to succeed in both political or economic prosperity. Leaders must acknowledge that North or South we are Nigerians first and foremost. We must speak with one voice so as to succeed in our collective efforts to bring sanity and prosperity in the country. It is a difficult task but it is a task that we must all strive at and ensure the success of oneness.

Leaders must lead by open-door policy with the public and continuous explaining of government objectives to the people will help build and sustain public trust. The media must work in collaboration with able leaders to create public support for government policies.

Government must invest in public programs that will jump-start economic prosperity in every local government area in the federation. Economic reforms in its entirety without investment on the Nigerian people will not bring economic prosperity.

As much as fundamental economic reforms are needed, compassion and investment on the people of Nigeria is of paramount importance. The economic prosperity of the 1970's led the nation into bad spending habits that did not encourage savings for the future. No serious thoughts were given to savings for the future generations to enjoy and be proud that they are citizens of Nigeria, instead with the oil boom came economic, political and leadership doom. Government began cash and spend habits that now runs through the fiber of every Nigerian. Because the government did not focus its insights on savings for the future, the economic fabric of the nation collapsed due to spend-thrift attitudes of leaders that could not see beyond their immediate environs and knew nothing about investing on the future.

142

Due to political expediency, short-term reliefs were always taken to deal with long-term pains. The problems faced by Nigerian leaders today are far greater than those of oil-boom era. Due to economic down-turn in the country, the leaders today are faced with a higher crime rate, selling and using of illegal drugs, inadequate public schools and extremely poor quality-of-life.

Suffice it to say that the ultimate success of economic prosperity and good quality-of-life depends squarely on the individual and the private sector, but to ensure this prosperity, the government must provide safe and clean cities, affordable and attractive public transportation, a foreign investment-friendly environment, a high-class thriving social society, services at airports, rail stations and bus terminals that are friendly to travelers. The government needs to get partnership agreements between huge corporations and universities in the area of technology. The public and private sector must work on the same goal to achieve adequate housing in the nation, the government can not do it alone neither can the private sector, hence it must be a two-way street. Strong leadership must encourage fundamental changes to improve the long-term economic prospects of the country. Increased investment on infrastructure should be encouraged not only in Abuja, Lagos or Kaduna but in all metropolitan areas of the country. An agenda in developing all urban and sub-urban areas in the country is needed immediately by every leader regardless of what ethnic group you belong.

Most of the problems facing Nigeria is self-inflicted and partly due to irresponsible leadership. Good federal leadership must deal effectively with national problems like the astronomical rate of poverty, high crime rate and hunger.

Leaders must appreciate the importance of developing

more cities in the federation and also developing more local government areas so as to increase economic prosperity of the nation. The country can not afford to fail in her bid to develop the hinterlands of the nation and this can only be achieved largely by individuals and the private sector, but with ultimate assistance from the federal government.

Economic prosperity is a long-term process and must be envisioned for the future with clear objectives and planned properly. It is time the North and South discarded the long heritage of mistrust and misunderstanding between each other, it is time to consolidate ideas and the entire people and develop into one ---- a leadership class of true oneness.

One of the true ways also for economic growth is for the North and South to invest simultaneously in each other. The blending of economies and the people of both North and South will ultimately establish a revolution of historic proportion that will only move the country forward and doing the opposite brings retrogression in the nation. The marriage of two fortunes makes a bigger and better profit. The strong forces of integration between all ethnic groups should persist and bring about a true legacy of one Nigeria.

Leaders must ensure political transformation that must be associated by gigantic shift towards a full-blown economic liberalization policies. Foreign investors must be welcomed with open-arms, strong incentives must be given to investors and private industries must assist government with technological know-how.

Economic prosperity must bridge the old gap between the South and the North and most especially between the rich and the poor. Government and foreign investors must invest on the rural dwellers and those who are economically and politically dispossessed both in the North and in the South.

Government and foreign investors must look after the well-being of the poor. Government and the private industry need Nigeria's best and brightest in leadership positions in the nation's quest for economic prosperity and political stability.

With all the human and mineral resources that Nigeria is blessed with, yet due to mismanagement and lack of compassion, the people of the country are faced with massive unemployment, petulant malnutrition, scarce education and an alarming deterioration of public services -- (i.e. electricity, water, telecommunication, etc) all these factors in large part have produced wide-spread disillusionment for the leadership of the nation.

Leaders have to lead by example and inculcate in the people that without economic and political reforms nothing can be done to improve the quality of life of the poor people.

If politicians lead with gusto and compassion and set good standards of leadership, eventually the military coups and military governments that had dominated the ruling class for decades will stagger toward destruction.

The civilian leaders that the country has, had inclination to be aging populist politicians from the 1960 and 70s and cautious of Nigeria's experience, they continue to maintain the prevailing economic policies of "government must control and command everything". The ultimate result has been greater economic disaster. The nation needs young prudent leaders with fresh ideas.

Massive corruption by government officials has contributed to the disillusionment of millions of Nigerians about their leaders. Many of the past leaders are now very wealthy beyond their wildest imaginations and they do not give back to the community.

Nigerians control billions of dollars of liquid capital in the Nigeria diaspora. The power of the Nigerians overseas will continue to increase and they will be the key players in the future of Nigeria but first they must shed their selfish-interests. Nigerians overseas must be energetic, risk-taking and networking individuals for the engineering of an economic prosperity for the nation. Nigerian people should have the basic tools for citizenship --- sobriety, literacy and employability. The country can not continue to sustain Northern dominance to the detriment of the Southerner.

In Nigeria, there are twice as many Southerners graduate from university than there are jobs available, but for Northerners, there are more jobs available than there are university graduates.

Decades ago, it looks as if gaining admission to a university was all any Nigerian student would need to get a good job after graduation. Today, the story-line is different, your ethnic background plays a key role.

Most of the Southern graduates who roam the street daily without success in getting employment are really bright and qualified and it seems such a colossal waste of human resources. These unemployed Southern graduates ask themselves ---- why did they attend a university for four years?

A Southerner should not be hostile toward the Northerner, because a Southerner who can agree and be friendly toward a Northerner does not make that Southerner a defender of the status quo.

At this stage of Nigeria's independence, a true leader can

146

not accept the conventional solutions of the old establishment. A true Nigerian leader must categorically oppose a political system in Nigeria where tribal issues are still overwhelmingly in debate in the entire political system.

There is a tendency in the South to question the validity of the successes of other Southerners. This tendency remains strong in the Southern community till present. Most successful Southerners are continuously confronted with it. The air of envy is very much around the successful Southerner. Neighbors resent him or her, even relatives cast aspersions to each other.

Leaders must teach their fellow Nigerians to abhor resentments or hatred and lay emphasis on rebuilding the nation through sacrifice and love for one another. Both Southern and Northern Nigerians must realize that human nature, both the good and the bad, knows no tribe or ethnic barrier. North and South both are capable of mysterious great kindness or cruelty. Within the Northern community which is often painted as unified against Southerners, there is also a great deal of tribalism based on ethnic, religious background.

The notion that Northerners caused all the political troubles are false. Southerners must accept some responsibilities for the political turmoil in the nation.
A true Nigerian leader can not and must not be fundamentally classified as -- Northerner, a Southerner, a Muslim, or a Christian leader. A true Nigerian leader must transcend religion or ethnic inclination. A true leader must spur Nigerians to look beyond themselves, they should get involved economically and politically and use their skills to aid others in the community.

Leaders must inspire the people to rethink their values

and look forward to the future with great vigor. The nation and her leaders have to come to grip with the reality that the old answers no longer work, instead they often add to the economic and political woes of a demoralized nation. The nation needs new solutions to adapt to the changing times.

Leaders in the past divert their attention from nation building and the enormous task of developing the rural areas, instead they increased their opportunities in politics and advancement of their economic liberation.

There is an increased psychological toll on the poor people of Nigeria, knowing that they can not participate in the political, economic and social life of the nation. The people feel that the political structure of the country is far removed from them and really out of their control. If these trend continues unabated, future generations would have no sociological or geopolitical sense of belonging in the country.

The saga of Nigeria's on-going internal argument over the role of personal faith in public life of the Presidency is insurmountable. There is a slim but strong wall that must separate matters of religion and government in Nigeria. The government's role on religion in the public life of the Presidency must be one of neutrality. The religion question is debated, fiercely and frequently across the entire nation.

Most Southerners claim or suggest that the Northerners always prefer the Head-of-state/President to be a Muslim, while in the South it does not matter what religion the Head-of-state/President belongs, hence the enormous clamor in the South for separation of state and religion. The North is viewed by Southerners as a symbol of religious intolerance. Some people on the fence would only claim that it is only the conservative Northerners who are intolerant of religious diversity. Liberals in the North and South want a legacy of religious freedom in public and private, but ultimate neutrality in the Head-of-state/Presidency. Religion belongs at home, church and mosque not in the Presidency. Some die-hard Islamic and Christian fundamentalists in the country fear a moral collapse if the Presidency is not compelled to some kind of religious adherence.

Nigeria is currently in the midst of religious agitation. The nation currently has an official Muslim/Christian establishment, but dissenters of other religious faith outnumbers Muslim/Christian adherents, because even in the Islamic/Christian communities there are various denominations e.g. in the Christian faith there are Anglicans, Baptists, Methodists, Catholics, Celestials, Aladuras etc.

The separation of religion and state must ensure liberty. The government and the Presidency must exercise no preference among religions but support all of them. The Head-of-state/Presidency must not be seen to favor one religion over another. Refining Nigerian thought on religious freedom from the state apparatus is a must. The nation must not accept any official religion. The federal government must be prohibited from establishing an official religion.

The duties of the people is that of vigilance in preference to secrecy, deliberation in preference to dispatch. Over the past decade, crime has become one of Nigeria's major exports. Flurries of bad publicity resulting from a string of drug trafficking to credit card fraud.

One of the supreme virtue that must be possessed by a leader is political courage. Some people think the key to acquiring wealth and influence in Nigeria is to be appointed into a public office.

The most popular perception in and outside the country is

149

that Nigeria is a fabulously wealthy nation, rich in mineral resources, but the country has eroded economically despite her oil riches due to mismanagement and self-aggrandizement by failed leaders.

Political and economic reforms must not be protracted. Leaders in government must set policies aimed at healing the ailing economy and also attack with great strength the entrenched corruption of government officials. Every government's most powerful opposition is no longer the South, the North, the Muslim or Christian but the entire poor masses of Nigeria.

Every government and leadership should be built from the bottom up and not destroyed from the top down. Nigeria is yet to witness a true democracy, instead what we have seen in the past is true hypocrisy. The money we spend on the military should be spent on industries and economic relief for the Nigerian people. Nigeria and Nigerian government must change and respond to changing circumstances. Power should not be concentrated exclusively in the hands of the military establishment.

No religion should stand-by and accept the tyranny of the majority. The potential threat to the nation that emanates from religious intolerance is enormous. The phantom of political crisis emerges of a nation chronically divided between a politically thriving North and a politically some-what backward South.

So far, many Nigerians at home and abroad have the pessimistic view that the situation in the country will not improve. The optimistic Nigerians believe that the federal government should deviate from an economy supported by government spending-spree to an economy of prudent management for the future of the nation.

For decades now, Nigeria has not succeeded in resolving the "Southern question" in the political process of the Presidency. Despite the economic woes of the country, the federal government still takes funds from the oil-rich South to the agricultural-based North. The South is economically different --- filled with huge business conglomerates and many small businesses. The Northern economy has been copiously contingent on agriculture and the political structure of the Presidency/Head-of-state.

North-South comparisons are dramatically rampant. In the Northern region, unemployment is low, while in the South, unemployed university graduates roam the streets. To some cynics, the South is simply being ignored, but the result of this neglect could be devastating in the future if not now.

In the South, while masses of youths suffer with no clear end in sight, the political leaders in the federal government are only interested in solving their personal financial situations. For now, survival in the Southern part of the country brings out the worst talents of improvisation from the impoverished people. The unemployed are not all sitting idle around doing nothing. Criminal activity is enjoying an enormous boom.

Armed robbery has increased on a massive scale, illicit drug trade is on the up-swing, car-snatching has also increased. For the less-skilled in the South, one of the few roads to follow is crime. For the skilled in the South, a vigorous migration wave to Europe and the United States has also increased. This situation has brought grave social tensions.

The country now needs leaders who dream of something other than filling their own bank accounts. Leaders who have compassion for the people. Leaders that will lead by good example. Leaders with a vision for prosperity.

Ethnic-based politics backed by money or military power has been very devastating in the country. A Nigerian, North or South has no value in his or her religion, education or social standing if armed with any of the above yet neither of these aroused compassion nor conscience. People in the country have allowed a need for status to over-rule common-sense. Presently, no one can count on the federal government to take care of them in their youth (or worst) neither in their old age.

Nigeria must be driven forward to economic and political stability with hope, but must not be taken backwards by fear and incessant political crisis.

Today, many Nigerians, feel that long-term security, once an expectation, is getting harder and harder to achieve. One of the important facet of security --- financial security -- is viewed by many Nigerians as impossibly out of their reach. Most people feel so insecure because they have lost faith in the federal government. Nigerians are used to their leaders "quick-fix" prescription to economic and political dilemmas of the country, but what the people want is long-term solutions to all the problems they have faced since the nation's independence.

The problems with moving forward economically in the country are clear to everyone. Most Nigerians strive everyday with the same issue: How to build financial security in a nation that is economically and politically insecure. The solution for the country and the people -- is taking personal control and responsibility.

Taking control means the leaders and the people must make crucial economic decisions. Nigeria and Nigerians are the biggest factor in solving their economic challenges. With Nigeria and Nigerians at the center of their economic security, only Nigeria and her citizens understand their dreams and aspirations.

Economic independence and political independence are inexplicably inter-twined, you can not have one and lose the other. Nigerian leaders and the people must be taught the basic principles of how money works -- principles that can mean the difference in their present discomfort/comfort and future economic security/prosperity. The nation and the people must put up with the pain of economic discipline with compassion now or the ultimate pain of economic disaster later. It is time to act prudently, if the nation's leaders want the country's future to be secure, free of anxiety and political crisis.

The nation and the leaders must decide today, where they want to be 5, 10, 15 years from now economically and politically. Decision on this vital answer must be made immediately and moving in that direction is the first step. Without economic prosperity, the necessities of life --- food, shelter and clothing --- as well as the luxuries of life are simply not possible. The despicable act of mismanaging the economy of Nigeria has brought pathetic ruins and poverty to the nation and her citizens.

So many Nigerians live in poverty, despite the clear fact that the country is enormously rich in mineral resources and human resources. Nigeria's economic security in the future should be paramount in the minds of every Nigerian. The embodiment of economic prosperity must be the personification that binds Nigerians together. The nation and the leaders must invest for the future of Nigeria and Nigerians.

153

Debt management is one of the most important ways to assure economic health. The nation must manage her debt, so as to achieve economic security. The nation's huge debt creates a cash drain and robs the country from the money needed to build a solid foundation for the future.

Most of the money accrued from the sale of crude oil is currently used to service the nation's debt, but prudent debt management is needed to facilitate processing of future loans for the development of the entire country.

For economic prosperity to stand the test of time and succeed effectively, leaders and every government functionary must work for the interest of the country not for the short-sighted, opportunistic and selfish manner that has been the personification of government functionaries in the past and almost present.

To the amazement of the Nigerian people, different classes of people have ruled the country yet rather than progress the nation is retrogressing to the brink of economic collapse.

The people of Nigeria are mostly concerned when they remember and look-around them and see that university-educated people have held cabinet positions including highly regarded well-respected professors, yet the nation has not improved in all spheres of life, the people often times conclude that, may be this is what is meant to be.

Turning the issues over, one can ascertain that university degrees has nothing to do with good and effective leadership. One of the greatest and one of the most effective American Presidents -- President Harry Truman, was not a university graduate. The solution is not military, politician, graduate or illiterate, the solution is leadership with commitment to nation and her citizens, honor, duty, service and most of all compassion. The solution also needs dedication and hard work.

Every Nigerian has a civic stake in the economic outcome of Nigeria. Saving Nigeria from political and economic oblivion is not complaining or criticizing the government or any one person, it is a collective responsibility of every Nigerian period.

WHAT NIGERIANS MUST DO

Nigeria need a leader with an activist agenda for rural development and creation of jobs.

Nigeria needs a pragmatic leader.

Nigeria needs a man or woman of unimpeachable authority.

Nigerians must not lose the capacity for respect, deference and trust.

Nigerians must have faith in their destiny and confidence in their future.

Nigerians must respect authority, be it the president, teacher or a policeman/policewoman.

Nigeria needs leaders with energy and new ideas, leaders who can speak out for those who need strong support --- the poor, the lonely and the weak.

Nigerians must be able to get beyond what divides Nigerians. Nigerians must stop embracing ethnic politics.

Nigeria needs innovators, ---- men and woman whose ideas and leadership will improve Nigerian schools, businesses and government.

Nigeria needs reform and hope for a better future.

Nigeria needs born leaders --- leaders who are poised and outgoing with a wide winning smile.

Nigeria is desperately in need for change, also security and welfare is of the utmost concern.

Nigerians (and Africans as a whole) need to get more of her people to care for one another.

Nigerians need a culture of tolerance, live and let live, civil society and protection of human dignity.

Nigerians need freedom to shape their future.

The federal government has to realize that the Nigerian people will make or brake the country, hence the government must be nice to her people and recognize the monumental fact that it is commitment, not authority that produces results.

The federal government and the private sector must help workers boost their skills.

The federal government should prove to be fiscally prudent and investor-friendly. It has to reject punitive taxation of the rich.

The federal government has to get a handle on the ever-increasing criminal violence.

The federal government must create social, political and economic reforms for the poor people of Nigeria.

The federal government should be willing to create opportunities for the people but the people themselves and their communities must also take responsibility for their growth and actions.

The federal government and state governments should work for the people not against the people.

The federal government must help the people to equip themselves to solve their problems.

Most leaders agenda has not been political revolution but social and personal redemption. All leaders agenda for the destiny of the Nigerian people should evolve into a land of peace, community, altruism, ethnicity-free and classless harmony.

With international aid fading from view, leadership's own financial planning efforts will continue to play an enormous part in determining the quality of the future of Nigeria. To circumvent a continuous decline in the standard-of-living of Nigerians, leadership must be prudent in planning and be committed to savings for the future. The wisest path is to expect the worst and save until it hurts and be pleasantly surprised if things turn out to be better than expected.

Due to strong and compassionate leadership, one man (Lee Kuan Yew) took a tiny country --- Singapore (population 3 million) that is entirely lacking in natural resources and turned it into one of the most prosperous places on earth. Per capita income far exceeds England's; there is very little crime, practically no unemployment and it has a first-rate educational system. All these occurred in a country that came out of world war 2 in ruins and destitute.

The crucial reason for the economic success in Singapore is the people, --- who are disciplined, take education seriously -- especially mathematics, science and engineering -- and also have cultural habits of extremely high savings and high investments and most important, always working for the next generation.

Nigeria has the prospect not only of becoming an economic superpower, but also of becoming a political and military superpower as well, but only through the path of compassionate leadership.

In every community in Nigeria, people do not have to move from one region to the other; what the people, the community and the government need to do is improve the living conditions and living standards of every community in the country.

The power of partnership is stability. The military and civilians, the Northerners and the Southerners must form an everlasting partnership in order to bring stability to the country. The way to the future is not only through the past but the present. Leadership must be on the pulse of tomorrow's problems today with solutions.

A leader needs the support and resources necessary to get the job done. The growing inequality in the country is not necessarily a sign of economic failure but leadership failure. Also what really matters is whether there are opportunities for people to move up the economic ladder, irrespective of where they start or what part of the country they come from.

Nigeria has become a nation polarized between the privileged rich and permanently poor. Leadership must take a provocative look at today's compelling economic problems.

As a leader, the more successful you are (especially in the South) the more likely you are a target of vicious personal abuse. Leadership and politics are becoming very acrimonious in Nigeria. But present and future leaders should not be daunted.

For the moment, Nigerian leadership is enjoying the sunshine and ignoring the clouds. Southern Nigerians should start investing on people by building lives through education

160

and hard work -- not blaming people. Leadership should reach out and help people to help themselves.

As a leader (or just an ordinary citizen), your determination and belief (not money and power) are enough to help people in need. The people are both confused and concerned that the massive amounts of federal budget stays at the top and not trickling down. Majority of the people are getting poorer and poorer. Part of what is wrong in Nigeria is that the North and South are too divided, they are not connected. Nigerians can not solve the bigger problems unless they solve the basic problems, and that is by caring for each other regardless of what part of Nigeria you are from. To solve these problems, it takes people not government. We can not solve community problems without community involvement and community empowerment.

Financial privacy is God-given right that the federal government should respect and not hinder. The Nigerian people want to accumulate wealth and they want to keep it. But the military leadership it seems, has an interest in keeping Southerners from accumulating wealth.

For decades, Nigerian politics stopped at the river Niger as Nigerians rallied against threats to Nigeria's existence as a federal entity. Now the united front is cracking, stressed by deep divisions over peace and unity.

It is often said that no person can do everything, but together we can do anything. And that is clearly what Nigerians (North and South) must realize. The North can not lead the nation alone, neither can the South continue on the path of followership without participation in leadership.

Food prices these days are so high. In fact, the price of everything is high, while the actual buying power of the Naira

161

is always falling. Life itself literally should be a pleasing progression where now should be better than before; days with possibilities to look forward to rather than certainties to shrink from. Nigeria is now a country of deepening cynicism and pessimism about its leaders, its institutions, its citizenry and its future, it has become culmination of a discouraged and mistrustful place. The peoples dream of equal opportunity, personal freedom and social/economic mobility has become farther out of reach in the past decade. Every nation have times that are awful, it is how the nation comes back from awful times that matters.

The defining characteristic of pessimists is that they tend to believe bad events will last a long time. The optimists, who are confronted with the same hard knocks of this universe, think about misfortune in the opposite way. The optimists tend to believe that defeat is just a temporary setback, a little bump on the road to success, not a major accident, that its causes are confined to just this one case. The optimists believe defeat is not their fault; circumstances and bad luck brought it about. The optimists do not look at how things are, they look at how things can be.

The United States of America was built on hard work, hope, faith and the dream that anyone can become successful. That is the promise of America. What is Nigeria built on and what is the promise of Nigeria? These are crucial questions that need accurate answers. The entire people of Nigeria must ensure that tomorrow's generation will profit from the errors and sacrifices of today's. The military has kept an iron grip on Nigeria -- intimidating, jailing and executing opponents of the military regime. Compassion comes from feeling another person's pain. Until leaders (military or civilian) start to feel the people's pain, "compassion" in Nigeria will continue to be just another big English word. The people of Nigeria can not, must not settle for what they were but what they will become. Most people are astounded to see how deeply Nigerian society continue to run adrift, despite the nation's laws and lips service to equality. The country is shaped by issues of wealth, ethnicity, geography and above all --- social class.

The people of Nigeria continue to fear that a permanent stay of the military in leadership position could jeopardize Nigeria's agonizing transformation into a "normal" country. The day and time Nigeria gets back to a normal society with freedom, justice and equality for all will be a defining moment for the country and the people to rise from poverty and pain to prosperity and greatness. The Nigerian people must place greater value and emphasis on what they contribute to society rather than on what they accumulate.

Despite enormous attacks on the federal government, an active federal government is not merely inescapable but necessary and even desirable. In any human community, especially in one as large, diverse, complex and contentious as Nigeria, federal government is and should be the institution that draws the people together, maintains order and advances the common interest of the people. No other institution can do this, hence the federal government must not merely exist but have the support of the entire people. The federal government not only has the potential to better society, it has a moral obligation to do so. Made in Nigeria makes Nigeria work. If Nigerians buy made in Nigeria, the economy improves and the people gain the benefits of made in Nigeria.

Right now, there is a stunning economic boom in Asian countries. Almost all the nations of that region have economic growth rates higher than the African nations, including enormous lower rates of crime, drug use and social ills. The secret of their success is "values". Asian societies constantly teach traditional moral values ---- in the temple church, mosques and in schools. But in contrast in today's Nigeria, obnoxious and insulting behavior has become acceptable, ostentatious displays of wealth are as good as exhibitionistic displays of one's religion/ethnic origin; more so, since fame is more highly valued than shame in Nigeria, we now have our role models wrong. At a time when Nigerians find drug dealers, corrupt public servants and criminals endlessly fascinating, the idea of being a pillar of the community/family sounds like a crude joke.

The federal government must be a positive force in the lives of the people.

The federal government should not forget the poor masses in the government's pursuit of economic development.

The federal government should stop serving itself and the economic elite, the government should start serving the Nigerian people and putting the Nigerian people first not last.

In order to ensure astounding quality of life, leadership and the people must have a shared commitment to business growth, cultural enrichment and preservation of the nation's natural beauty. True to the old adage that "location is everything", Nigeria is blessed by its position in Africa. Nigeria offers over 100 million consumers, hence, foreign investors must take advantage of the market and create a strong, financial, corporate and manufacturing center. Location is not the only factor that will encourage business and the Nigerian economy to grow; the leadership and the entire Nigerian community must be pro-business because workers are plentiful, also wages must be competitive. Economic development to create employment opportunities in every community in the nation (not only by the federal government but by the private sector) is an indispensable element of the Nigerian society, by matching talents and expertise with the vision, community leaders, business leaders, military leaders and political leaders to address the issues of importance to the quality of life of the "giant of Africa".

Leadership must bring together researchers and corporate leaders from the private sector, governmental agencies and university to provide a mechanism to integrate technological results from research into private corporate programs for public use. For Nigeria, the future of economic development has never been brighter. Leadership must now bring a wide range of employment and business opportunities to millions of people in Nigeria. Leadership must always emphasize to the private sector that the community where a business is located owes you (the business) nothing, it is up to you the business to go out and earn the community's respect. Every business has a corporate responsibility to make the community where the business is located a better community. Business performance is and will continue to be phenomenal for all those involved in the future of Nigeria as she will shine as the best of the best in Africa.

Change is good but critics of change are simply trying to protect failing military leadership and the old political leadership. The agony of the past is outweighing the promise of the future. Civilization has always been equated with industrialization, and progress is defined as the accumulation of capital and the proliferation of industrial inventions. Rewards for the wealthy, the productive and the innovative is the key to technological advancement and economic improvement in Nigeria.

Tearing down governmental barriers to change, will accelerate the arrival of a high-technological information age with unparalleled possibilities for the Nigerian society. This will fulfill Nigeria's destiny of becoming an economic giant

165

not a population giant.

I repeat, military regimes in Nigeria have always believed that democratic electoral politics is bourgeois and a rigged process of the elite rich class. They believe that the only way to stop the process is to shut down the machine by coups and counter-coups. The Nigerian people always envisage that the military wants to bring about change with the barrel of a gun.

The M.K.O. Abiola-led election annulment by General Ibrahim Badamasi Babangida is a misguided tragedy that has not served the national interest but also does not warrant the spilling of a single Nigerian blood.

One of the most important requisite of a free society is a free economy not government regulations. Economic controls are the virulent cancer of federal government power. A free and good society is best served by a smaller, less activist federal government and by a more dynamic, productive and fluid market place. The iron-clad society created by the military is not accountable to the people because the instruments of government have been seized to serve the parochial ends of the military elites and their cronies. Military might has become might. Public policy is no longer high-minded nor an ideological endeavor by the military.

In a political administration, before the federal government can redistribute wealth, the society must first produce it, but in a military administration, the federal government distributes wealth to the military elites whether society produces wealth or not. Nigerians must realize that they now live in an era not of limits but of limitless possibilities. Capitalism is endlessly resourceful. If the Nigerian people have enough incentives, prosperity is inevitable.

Nigeria must be started anew. Nigeria's current accumulating economic and social breakdowns must be repaired and her older ills of tribalism and poverty must be vanquished by sweeping changes in the policies that caused or prolonged them. The destructive notions of scarcities, catastrophes, economic limits, incurably embedded inflations and avoidable financial breakdowns that had by now come to enthrall most administrations must come to a screeching halt. The Naira must be made stable again by fixing its value to a constant quantity of real economic goods. Economic and moral regulation by the government must stop immediately.

Most administrations are supposed to stimulate investments, jobs and economic growth, but, instead what they normally do is build up governmental power and economic inefficiency. Thus creating a situation where the country and her people now have too few money chasing too few goods.

It is the indiscipline of politicians and military administrators that continues to threaten the integrity of the nation's money. The nation needs sound money, capitalist prosperity, social mobility, entrepreneurial dynamism and individual incentives.

Inflation in the country has become a monetary phenomenon caused by the policies of the central bank of Nigeria and also an economic disorder caused by businesses and investors. Due to bad leadership, everything in the country is supposedly getting attention but nothing is getting priority. Meanwhile, the economic situation is worsening by the day, thus making most administration's essential job --- restoring non-inflationary prosperity. Nigeria's potent enemy is time.

The nation's national policy should be nurtured, shaped,

screened, debated, refined and virtually resolved before full implementation. Nigeria's governance should also be profoundly transformed. The nation can not afford to continue with the astounding triumph of the ideology of a few over the political necessities of the many. National policy must be built on ideas (of majority of the people) not power (by a few people).

Most military administrations have the idea that implies that the government owns all your income and has the right to decide what you can keep and also question how you made your income. The nation needs leadership with challenge and creativity. Leaders must realize that you do not throw money at problems, you find solutions to problems.

Leadership must reward private investors, entrepreneurs and investors. The entire economic future of Nigeria depends on rapid technological advance and this must come from the private sector not the government. Technological advancement is a gift of the marketplace, not of government bureaucracies. Leadership must not impose political solutions on economic problems.

Most administrations have continued to defer Nigeria's economic and political problems rather than solve the fundamental issues. The country continues to be in a threshold faced with a question of hope versus Nostalgia. Would Nigerians go with a brave new leadership or stick with the failed leadership of the past? That is what Nigerians must finally be called upon to decide. The nation is a little behind of schedule politically and a little behind schedule financially. Things are not looking grand on the political/economic side, thus the people are naturally following these developments with a clear reaction ----- panic. This generation needs compassionate leadership ----- if not us, who? If not now, when? The country does not need a leader who is just an advocate for the wealthy or the military but utterly insensitive to the needs of the common Nigerian.

The country can not continue to take a giant leap backward in order to take a giant leap forward, we must take a quantum leap forward for the immediate and the future, period. The country does not need a leader with the ideals of the Northerner or the vision of a Southerner, the country needs a Nigerian leader for the entire Nigerian people --- North, South, East or West. The betterment of the common Nigerian does not depend exclusively upon the largesse of the federal or state or local government, it includes the potent private sector. Redistribution of wealth by the private sector and the government is not the problem but the solution.

The military administrations have continued to be dedicated to socialist wealth redistribution, while the politicians are dedicated to capitalist wealth creation. Capitalism is the by-product of capitalists. It is the rewards that drives invention, innovation and entrepreneurial risk taking --- it produces intellectual capital, which in turn brings about more out-put and wealth from the farms and factories. Nigerian leaders and the people must stop the politics of envy --- the deliberate inciting of the middle-and-lower-class resentment of the rich and famous.

Past leaders brought more politics than vision to the role they assume in the office of the Presidency-or Head-of-State. Governance to the past leaders is not a realm of pure reason, analysis and the clash of ideologies. It is the involvement of brute force of personality, the effrontery of bloated egos and the raw will of power.

Past leaders feel that the raw hunger for power is as important a part of the equation as pure ideas; hence the field of past leadership was full of inflamed egos, maneuvering purely for the sake of power and status. A leader's vision must not be obscured by ideology. Every leader (both civilian and military) must realize that winning any battle per force means losing the war itself. The elements at play in Nigerian leadership crisis includes the natural jealousy and mutual suspicion between the military and the politicians. The military and the politicians accuse each other of greed and corruption. The military and the Northerners do not want to be in a capacity as participants rather than principals in the office of the Presidency/Head-of-State, while the Politicians and the Southerners want to be principals rather than participants in the office of the Presidency or Head-of-State.

Military administrations have continued to guarantee half-revolution and fiscal disaster. The nation's economic policy has always been in the hands of undetermined and ineffective leadership that never knew what it wanted and how to get it. The only way to achieve fiscal prosperity is for compassionate leadership to make strategic choices and fundamental choices. Leadership must cure the high-inflation, low-growth economy of Nigeria.

History is well and fine. The nation must not be confused and concerned with the past because what confronts the nation of Nigeria is the future. The country has arrived at the bitter pill hence the leaders must not fail to establish that the patient is ill. The question must stop to be what could be done and become what should be done.

Government must stop indicting the innocent poor people and rewarding the guilty and the rich. Government must disinflate the economy and stimulate production. Reality shows that leadership can not ultimately promise instant, painless economic redemption from all the cumulative danger, disorder, excesses and imbalances that has been embedded in the Nigerian economy due to prior bad leadership.

The military and Northerners must not continue to project an image of an occupied state to politicians and Southerners who wants them to be neighbors and One Nigerian Family. The economic recovery and the future of Nigeria is at stake. North and South, military and politicians must come together now.

A President or Head-of-State should be a leader not a dictator. A leader must know that Nigeria has an open future of limitless possibilities. A compassionate leader must also know that defeats are not permanent facts but merely temporary, reversible disappointments. A leader must not rule by confrontation but by consensus. A leader must not also allow political advice to overwhelm economic analysis. The people of Nigeria have realized that strong and compassionate leadership is the key to prosperity and the lack of it meant trouble for everyone, including both military and political leaders, hence they turned to Dodan Barracks or Aso Rock not to throw rocks but to ask, in earnest what the game plan is and was now.

Past leaders have misled the country by a crew of overzealous and ultimately incompetent advisers. Past Presidents or Head-of-State chose to be not a leader of the entire nation but a politician and in essence they showed why passion and imperfection not reason and ideology rule the country. Their quest for power overshadows their reasoning.

The country needs a leader and leaders that will and can make tremendous decisions for the betterment of Nigeria's future. Due to bad leadership both by the military and politicians, Nigeria no longer have any revolution to betray, only a shambles to repair. The will of the Nigerian people is at drastic variance with the actions of the politicians and the military establishment. The country needs leaders that will bring to the task of the office of the Presidency --- a strong will, an incisive mind and a towering personality/credibility to see the job through.

A leader must have the comprehension that inflation is a profoundly destructive phenomenon. The future and the prosperity of Nigeria and Nigerians depends upon the fundamental health of the economy and soundness of fiscal policy.

There is absolutely no basis in economic history or political theory for believing that from the shaky foundation, a profound lasting era of economic/political prosperity can actually emerge.

Past leaders have sacrificed future living standards of Nigerians by turning the country into a debtor nation.

Past leaders did not display any patience, determination or ability in the governance of the country. Some leaders, General Muhammadu Buhari/Major General Tunde Idiagbon -- General Ibrahim Badamasi Babangida/Admiral Augustus Aikhomu, instead of launching War-on-Poverty, they launched War-against-Indiscipline aimed specifically at the civilian population.

The people of Nigeria have come to the profound and unmistakable conclusion that what counts is what the leadership did, not what the leadership intend. Leadership must realize that economic governance must consist of a fundamental trade-off between capitalist prosperity and socialist security. The nation and its leaders must not choose to have less of the former in order to have more of the latter.

Since the military elite started their so-called revolution

in the country based on coups and counter-coups, they have continued to kill civilians and military officers, they have almost exterminated the educated middle class in the South and they transformed Nigeria into a profound rural prison camp that works, starved and beat to death thousands of Nigerians. No one in Nigeria or outside Nigeria has satisfactorily explained what has and continues to drive the military to such grotesque extremes of torture and killings of the citizens they swore to defend and protect by their allegiance and oat of office.

The lust for total power by the military and their small circle of trusted comrades seem to control the entire country by brutal military force.

Nigeria is now in an era of tremendous internal tension between the rich and the poor, between the North and the South and most of all between the military and the politicians. The conflicts and uncertainties of today are a sign of failed leadership. The three barons of politics --- Balewa, Zik and Awolowo have thus far turned their personal battles into a struggle that has now permanently reshaped Nigeria.

The battle between General Ibrahim Badamasi Babangida/General Sanni Abacha and Chief Moshood Kashimawo Olawole Abiola tells us that ---- progress is literally yet another illusion of human beings. Human institutions change but human nature does not. The same tribalism problems that Nigeria and Nigerians faced in the era of Balewa, Zik and Awo is the same inherent ethnicity-based quagmire that Babangida/Abacha and Abiola has soaked themselves and Nigerians.

At best, it can be said that Nigerians and Nigeria take one step backward for every two steps forward; more appropriately, Nigeria and Nigerians take one step forward, one step backward --- hence they remain at the same place since independence. Because when you look at Nigeria deeply from the 60's to the 90's, the more things change, the more they remain the same.

Success must not be measured by that which was gained alone, success must also be measured by that which was overcome. Leaders must deeply respect reason, principles and the dispassionate search for truth. Leaders must also show a depth of allegiance to family, friends and the ONENESS of Nigeria. Leaders must be motivated primarily by friends, family, reason and rationality. A leader's public accomplishments must be rooted in his or her private self.

Due to bad leadership --- Nigeria today is a much changed Nigeria --- impoverished, stupefied and bleak. One of the greatest strengths about America (U.S.A.) is that you can come from a position of nothing or very little but aspire to be great and actually achieve that greatness.

In Nigeria, the nation and her people are confused and concerned but claim that they need a revolution in education of compassion. When the military took over power in Nigeria, since the General Muhammadu Buhari regime till date, the military leaders encouraged overseas Nigerians to come and help rebuild Nigeria --- "because we have no other country than Nigeria", they came -- and many of them have been killed or imprisoned. It is like the prodigal child in reverse ----- going back to a place that was hell and inflicted so much suffering on their own generation and the future generation. It is not like the parent forgiving the child ---- but the ultimate goal now is for the offspring to forgive the parent.

Many Nigerians despair that their government after years of expressing support for diversity and a mixed society, has continued to balk just when it has the chance to realize the ideals it claims (e.g. M.K.O. Abiola's election victory). Southerners/Christians claim that Northerners/Muslims talk brotherhood and unity, but in their hearts, Muslims/Northerners want their own nation. Muslims/Northerners do not want a united Nigeria because that means they will have to share POWER. Both Southerners/Christians and Northerners/Muslims must realize that whatever begins in anger ultimately ends in shame.

Although, most leader's enemies came almost entirely from their public life, but the passions of their time most seriously affects their private life.

The vision of a good Nigerian society rests on the strength and productive potentials of free Nigerians and free markets. This vision through compassionate leadership must encourage the unfettered production of capitalist wealth and expansion of private welfare not just federal and state government welfare.

Most administrations have continued to take from the people instead of giving to the people. After an enormous pillage of the economy by most administrations, recently, most administrations have continued with a sweeping and wrenching change in national governance that continues to hurt millions of people. These severance of economic prosperity has brought short-run pain in the name of long-run gain.

Since the oil-gloom era begun, most administrations brought economic blueprints that are riddled with hardship and unfairness of unexpected change. Leaders in the country forget that the people are the ones who have the LAST AND FINAL say.

Leaders must have a redeeming virtue. They must be willing to face economic and governance reality. Most administrations have continued to invent illicit enterprises of government that bleed the national economy.

Leaders must teach the people about the gratifying effects of farming. Growing up on a farm instills you with ambition. The results of your work are visible -- a field of ripening tomatoes, a farm painstakingly cultivated and maintained. These are the palpable things -- evidence that you can impose your will and ideas and have them come out according to your plan.

Leaders should be practical and cautious and must also teach the people to take things one step at a time. You must not leap before you look, instead look before you leap.

Christian fundamentalists believe that the rural areas cultivated morals and character, the big cities cultivate vice. They believe that smoking, drinking, gambling and violating the Sabbath is the way of fallen sinners; but temperate living and church-going are the mark of the saved and good Christians.

The questions people continue to ask and never seem to have a clear and profound answer are:- why do Nigerians hate the military regime? How does the media establishment undermine the military regime? What are the sources of discontent between the military regimes and the people? These are the central themes of contemporary Nigerian politics. Also, most crucial, perhaps, is the military leadership's failure to understand what the public wants. Hopefully with compassionate leadership and the will to make better things for better living, might and should bring us a little closer to the day when the federal government will work to improve the lives of the citizens of Nigeria it was designed to serve.

One of the most crucial problem facing the leadership of the military is that leaders often do not have time to learn the basics of leadership. The military has officers who shoot their way into leadership roles with little or no training. Just as with sports e.g. soccer has a coach or coaches that pushes soccer stars like Pele to excel so also military officers need training and trainers to make them become effective leaders, broaden their skills, tackle personal weaknesses and preserve a personal life.

Making the transition from a good military officer to a good leader is difficult but it should be the ultimate goal of every military officer, because while military officers deal with military issues, military leaders lead people. The focus on good leadership is; where is the country and the people, where does the country and the people want to go and how does the country and the people want to get there in the future.

As Nigeria lumbers to its feet as Africa's greatest untapped market, more Americans (students, business leaders and scholars) are aiming starry gazes directly at Africa, barely noticing Aso Rock trying to block their view. One of the biggest challenge for Nigerian leadership is not trade or troops but keeping Americans interested in Nigeria. Americans (it seems) have never bothered to learn what makes the Nigerian tick, and fewer Americans than ever seem interested. The lack of interest and understanding translate directly into lost profits for both countries. American corporations, government and media, at the very top levels, have almost nobody who really understands Nigeria, (despite the profound fact that Nigeria is one of the leading oil producers/exporters of oil to the United States and the most populous black nation on earth) and this leads to very bad judgements.

Nigerians are also fed a constant diet of American movies, music and fashion. Most Nigerians have some understanding of American culture and history. But most Americans can not name more than two cities in Nigeria -- Lagos and Abuja nor could they name any Nigerian leader in the past thirty (30) years. Some Nigerians conclude that the lack of interest simply results from Americans increasingly looking inward. But some Nigerians also blame much of America's declining interest in Nigeria on the Nigerians themselves. In essence, Nigerians are looking forward (with hope not fear) to the day when Aso Rock will look more like a destination and less like an obstacle to Americans.

Nigerian leaders must do more to improve people's daily lives. Leaders must help the Nigerian state onto the path of economic/political growth. To accomplish economic/political successes, leaders must curb inflation, privatize state-owned enterprises and establish a free market. The current social aspect of reform leaves much to be desired. Nigeria must produce more and the people must receive more. Leaders must put together all the things Nigeria needs for sustained growth, because the situation for ordinary people in the country is still profoundly very difficult. Nigeria's future prosperity lay in its rich oil production and in its rich soil for agricultural processing industries. Also further privatization in Nigeria will attract more foreign investment.

As a leader you must have a strong individual commitment to succeed and a willingness to make the necessary sacrifices to reach your goal.

Southerners are trying to get by terrorism whatever (including the Presidency) they could not gain by negotiations. Southerners and Northerners should be politically committed through compromise for a vision of a peaceful Nigeria dedicated to economic development rather than war.

Almost all of the federal government policy (in every administration --- civilian or military) is responsive instead of preventive. Leaders must know that when you change everything and you brake the rules, you expect the reactions and that is what happened in Nigeria between General Ibrahim Badamasi Babangida/Sanni Abacha and Chief M.K.O. Abiola. The military leadership changed everything in the political process and broke the rule of engagement with the Nigerian people hence the thunderous reactions from Nigerians at home and abroad.

Asian nations in general (e.g. Thailand) has been the recipient of most of the investment from rich industrial nations (especially the United States of America), accounting for almost sixty (60) percent of capital flows in the past decade. Thailand's growth is fast, its banking system is healthier and much of the capital that Thailand is importing is financing investment, not consumption. To the contrary, Nigeria and most third world countries import consumption instead of financing investments. Nigeria has been saddled with a troubled economy for years and is now looking for able leadership to stabilize the economy. Nigeria's economic problems seem localized but it is also globalized.

To be successful, you have to have a goal, if not, you are just treading water. You have to know where you are going --- or at least what you are intending, because, in the end, hard work is the true enduring characteristic of successful people and successful nations. Also, to be successful, a leader or a nation must not be daunted by fear of failure because failure itself is literally a step towards success. Fear of failure and failure itself is the fuel of achievement. If you are not afraid to fail, you probably would not be highly motivated to succeed. Failure is good but failing to try is very bad. Plans for economic growth by any leader must be fiscally prudent, publicly popular, philosophically and politically workable.

The ability of people (and countries) to transform themselves and find the courage to make decisions that will reshape their future is the most profound metamorphosis that is paramount to the people (or country's) prosperity. The journey not the arrival is the first principle. The quest (vision) is always more important than the accomplishments.

North and Southern Nigerians must end the decades of distrust and suspicion that divides them. It is time for North and South to unite together and return Nigeria to prosperity and greatness. In recent times, Southerners passiveness and lack of organization (due to greed and jealousy) have sent a loud and clear message to the leadership of the nation; that you can treat Southerners any way you want. You can deny Southerners access to capital needed to businesses and their communities. You can take jobs from Southerners, lock them up, accuse them of coup plotting and sentence them to death. You can do all these and more to Southerners in oil-rich Nigeria and yet there is absence of outrage at injustice by Southerners. If these trend continues, there will be no bright future for Southerners in Nigeria.

To guarantee a bright future for Southerners and the entire country, Southerners must have economic and social supports to build strong families, proud communities and a brighter country ---- Nigeria.

One of the advantages Northerners have is that -- they generally go to mosque every Friday, they always gather in one place (the mosque) and discuss religion and politics at the

180

same time, while Southerners and Christians generally do not attend church except for special occasions and in this special occasions as it is on every Sunday church service, religious topics are the norm while political discussions in church is a taboo, hence, for Northerners, Islam is a way of life, while for Southerners, Christianity is only a religion.

Leaders must take a provocative look at today's most compelling poverty rates. Leaders must also know that when you are comfortable you can do anything. We must see opportunities where others see obstacles. Leaders modus operandi should be hard work, self confidence and positive thinking. The nation needs thoughtful prudent investors and leaders. Business and political leaders should be aware of how their actions affect children and the future of Nigeria. Leaders must know that where there is no guts there is no glory. To build something that endures, it takes hard working people, people who care, people with vision and people with remarkable commitment.

Nigeria has suffered from division, famine and civil war. The military's rule of Nigeria is full of horrors. Most Nigerians however, assert that General Yakubu Gowon was the founder of Nigeria's greatness, which was later frittered away by his fumbling successors and so-called reformers. These people claim that during Gowon's regime, Nigeria and Nigerians were respected all over the world, but not any more. People insist that although there was squandering of wealth, during this time (Gowon's regime) but that most of the nation's money was used to build the infrastructures that are now in place today --- national stadium, Festac Town, federal highways etc. But today's leaders only know their pockets and their family's well-being. The country now has a culmination of a growing dissolution of military regime in the last years of this decade with administrative chaos and bitter personal animosities among top military/government

181

officials.

Electricity is the power that makes things better for better living, until Nigeria improves its power of electricity, the country can forget about car manufacturing, VCR's, TV sets, submarines, luxury cruise ships, steam boats, electric fans, air conditioners, telephones, faxes, computers -- oh computers ---- the essentials for today's industries and technologies, war ships, telescope, pianos, guitars, electric iron, metro rail, stereo sets, space development program i.e. going to the moon --- ah it is meant for only developed nations, our brains are too small to dream big and accomplish big things, we only seat and marvel at the development nation's achievements with oh ah isn't that wonderful. In Nigeria, our concept of electricity is for the functions of light to see day and night, to play stereo, to on/off the TV/VCR and for dance parties ---- that is all. What a limited function.

In this age of ferocious global competition, Nigeria's success or failure as a nation is going to be determined by knowledge, learning, information and skilled intelligence with compassionate leadership. Also who teaches tomorrow's children is vitally important ---- too important to leave to the vagaries of the military.

Nigeria's national economic security depends upon attracting the nation's best and brightest into teaching. Recruitment of teachers should be a national priority. To change Nigeria for the better, leadership must be a teacher.

A few decades ago, South Korea and Hong Kong were two of the poorest nations in the world. Right now they are among the richest. These two entities (South Korea and Hong Kong) became rich not by following the doctrines of development experts in the world, by releasing their people's energies not killing their people or giving their people long-term imprisonment. If the leadership create an environment where people are allowed to prosper, they usually will and the leadership and the entire country benefits.

Why is the Japanese Yen strong, the American Dollar strong, the British Pound strong but Russian Rubble is weak and Nigerian Naira is weak? The reason is not because of Japanese, American and British nuclear power, it is because of British, Japanese and American economic power. If Nigerians want the Naira to be strong, the leadership should plough all the billions of Naira of political transition into job creation, all the millions of Naira that are stolen through massive corruption should be used for job creation not building huge mansion and buying luxury cars and parking them in the garage. Every millionaire should use their millions to create jobs for Nigerians and turn the armed robbers into workers. Instead of retiring southerners left, right and center, jobs should be created for every Nigerian. When people work they can feed themselves and their family, the economy also improves, the Naira becomes strong and the nation will beam with pride. A nation that is always laying-off workers and not preparing them for another job opportunity is a nation that will ultimately breed armed robbers and hired assassins. A nation that do not pay her police officers and teachers regularly is a nation with irresponsible leadership. While a well-paid teacher will teach the Nigerian children (that are the leaders of tomorrow) moral values and good education, a well-paid police officer will protect every citizen against crime.

Too often, Nigerian leaders hold tightly to their peanut ideas for fear that they may lose them, when all the while, it is these very peanut ideas that holds the country and the people captive and prevent the freedom and prosperity the country and the people long for.

183

Corporations all over the world exist to produce things consumers want at competitive prices. Businesses in Nigeria should pay attention to the social welfare of their workers. The people of Nigeria are asking -- what are the social responsibilities of private companies to their workers, to the community where they operate and to the entire country? This is one of the nation's most enduring questions.

Construction business is a very big business in Kuwait because much of the country has had to be reconstructed in the years after the Persian gulf war. In Kuwait, money can quickly refurbish the past. To the contrary in Nigeria, with all the oil wealth, leadership can not refurbish the past and face the present in order to move forward to the future. In Kuwait, the leadership makes the oil wealth work for the citizen not against the citizens. From the day that you are born in Kuwait, everything is free -- delivery, special care, everything is free and the government of Kuwait starts to pay for you. The typical Kuwaiti child, who is born at government expense, among his or her life of government largess, free health care is just the beginning. If either of the child's parents work for the government, his or her birth means an immediate pay raise of $200.00 a month. At age 4, the child starts kindergarten, which is free, as is all education through Kuwait university. After he or she graduates, he or she goes to the civil service and finds a job waiting. All Kuwaiti university graduates are guaranteed a government job and after a year on the job, the person gets the standard seven weeks vacation. The government also gives the citizen $14,000.00 as a wedding gift. The government of Kuwait also builds the newlyweds a house or provides them $25,000.00 loan to build their own. But the house or loan is not free. The married couple must pay back this interest-free loan at the rate of $160.00 a month, which is a little less than the raise they will automatically get for each child they produce. And each of these children will instantly be eligible for the same benefits as their parents. But neither Nigerian children nor their parents (especially the Ijaws who produce the oil wealth in Nigeria) do not have a single benefit only horror from the moment they are born. While Nigeria uses her oil profits to build huge war machines/huge military institutions and slaughter each other, Kuwait's ruling family used their oil wealth to create a social welfare system.

Wealth is when small efforts produce large results. Poverty is when large efforts produce small results -- and this is literally what is happening in Nigeria.
One wonders, if it makes Nigerians feel safe and secure to know that every day the country and the people are getting poorer and poorer?

Leaders continue to avoid taking economic/political risks because they love security, forgetting that, if you avoid risk, you also avoid opportunity, because risk is the price you pay for opportunity. A leader can not hate risk and hope for prosperity. The North and the military should take a risk and give power to a Southerner and a civilian. Risk is an essential part of progress risk is also an essential step in the road to wealth.

Leaders must know that failure is part of success. A very important part indeed. If leaders develop a positive mental attitude about failure, a leader can learn a lot from failure. A leader will develop ingenuity, flexibility and an ability to create new ways of accomplishing goals.

Every person/leader has risen to the top of his or her field with some amount of failure. A person can not drown by falling in water, a person drowns by staying there. Failure is not bad. One good failure can teach you more about success. Failure can be the best thing that ever happened to Nigeria, its leaders and the people ---- the question is are they learning

185

from this failure so as to achieve success?

Nigeria's vision for the year 2000 and beyond, should start taking shape today. It is Nigeria's future and it must start today. Nigeria's economic growth is promising but above all the country needs leadership. Leaders must use the skills they have and develop the skills they need and want.

The Nigerian people (except the Igbo community) has ceased to assume personal responsibility for their financial well-being, they assume that the government is responsible for their financial well-being. While to the contrary, government is not the answer. The answer lies in self-reliance and personal responsibility.

The Nigerian people alone are responsible for their ultimate financial future. With prudent planning and patience, Nigeria and the people can become prosperous starting right from where they are now and achieve success in five years or less.

As architects of financial prosperity, leaders need to lay a solid foundation. Leaders must make Nigerian money to grow, because, as often as it is compelling, Nigerian leaders find it easier to spend the people's money than saving it. When choosing between sacrifice and instant gratification, the wealth seeker chooses sacrifice and the poverty seeker chooses instant gratification. The wealth seeker knows that if he or she can just wait and invest for the future, he or she can have anything and buy whatever he or she wants.

Nigerian leaders misused the people's money through ineptitude, dishonesty, bad luck or a combination of all three vices. Also, due to Nigerian leaders love for instant gratification, when it comes to foreign investment, it prefers "potato chips not computer chips ---- consumption not

186

production".

Like a fool and his or her money are soon parted, that is exactly what has happened to Nigeria, because Nigerian leaders do not understand the word "investment". Nigerian leaders do not understand leverage, compound interest or control. And as long as leaders do not pay a second thought about the task of preparation that go into most economic/political successes --- the sacrifices, the planning, the coordination, the sleepless nights and the prices paid. The ultimate journey from Nigeria's financial bondage to financial freedom is more like launching a satellite into orbit. To launch a spaceship, it takes careful planning and enormous coordination. Any leader wishing to launch Nigeria's financial spaceship into permanent orbit high above the fiscal monetary troubles of normal life and beyond the gravitational strain of inflation, taxes and mismanagement should be well prepared and well coordinated for it. But, also at the crucial moment of preparation and coordination, it is much better to have the entire country with you (the leader) than against you (the leader).

This is the time for Nigerian leaders to lick their wounds, swallow their prides and change directions. They have spent billions of Naira into the old ways and killed thousands of people during this process yet nothing good was achieved, it is time for leaders to change direction drastically.

Allow a Southerner/Christian to be the President or Head-of-State, this Southerner/Christian does not have to be Igbo or Yoruba, just like all the past leaders (President or Head-of-State) from the North did not come just from Sokoto or Kano. There are able leaders from Calabar, Ijaw, Isoko, Tiv, etc. But the question is will the military and the Northerner have the courage to change? Would the Yoruba or Igbo people step aside and allow the Ijaw, Isoko, Calabar, Tiv, etc. to assume leadership roles in the office of the Presidency or Head-of-State? These are the fundamental questions that leadership must answer. All these take sacrifice --- leadership is not willing to pay the price.

It seems Nigerian leaders prefer to die of thirst just inches from the water fountain. If not, why the continuation of the old ways of instant gratification? A nation's wealth is not in the budget speeches made by the President or Head-of-State. A big budget speech is nothing but hot air if there is no golden stream to refill the well where the money comes from. Leadership must now leave the realm of fiscal theory and enter economic reality. The only true path to success is through failure. Nigeria and its leaders have failed, it is now time to learn from the failure and achieve success both economically and politically.

North and South, christians and muslims, military and politicians must solve the country's problems in a mutually beneficial way. People must do unto others as they would have them do unto you. The North must not win and make the South lose and vice versa. The time has come when North and South should start to solve each other's problems and they must do this as partners instead of as adversaries. A true Nigerian, (North and South) must build an atmosphere of trust, honesty and understanding. It is only in this atmosphere that Nigeria's problems will be revealed and alternative solutions would be explored.

The North and South must trust each other, because when trust is destroyed, North and South would remain adversaries. And adversaries do not have any incentive to help each other. The North and South should be helpful to each other not abrasive, they must try to solve problems not intimidate each other, they must be part of the solution instead of part of the problem. You get out of any situation what you put into it. You reap what you sow --- hence if the North and South want the country and her people to succeed in economic/political process, they must put into the process what they want out of the process - economic/political growth or economic/political disaster.

A strong and compassionate leader is not shaken by financial collapse or catastrophe. It is only a weak leader and poverty-minded leader that jumps out of windows when they lose everything. A strong leader has the courage and ability to start all over again, because the only wealth and security lies in one's head -- to make the leader reason and come back stronger, richer and wiser. Now, the nation is calling on compassionate leadership to start the country all over again in the true path to success.

A strong and compassionate leader needs time, knowledge, people and courage to bring the country back on its feet once again. The nation and her leaders must have a goal to make a comeback in economic and political prosperity. The nation and its leaders must invest for the future. Investment is just another word for sacrifice. Sacrifice is the direct opposite of instant gratification ---- just like legacy is another word for love. All these means, sow now, reap later, sacrifice or invest now, enjoy the fruits later. But without a mutual understanding between the leadership and the people on what the country really wants/needs and what it will take to get it, the whole investment/sacrifice/legacy/love process is on a shaky foundation.

Every failure is valuable to those who persist and want to succeed. Half a cake is better than no cake at all, also better than a whole cake with blood and nails in it. It is time for North and South to share the leadership cake or have no cake at all or have a whole cake with blood and nails in it. The prescription medicine to attain this process must not be worse than the disease itself. It is the long-term possibilities of a cure that should excite the leaders and the people not the short-term cure with long-term devastation.

North and South must combine their limited talents and finances to make big things happen in Nigeria -- because there is strength in numbers. None of them, individually (North or South) could be successful alone, but together (North or South) it will be a piece of cake to achieve economic and political prosperity. There is nothing profoundly wrong with starting from scratch. Creating economic prosperity may take a little longer and require more sacrifice, but we can still get there (to the top of the mountain) from where we are now. We either start all over again or abandon ship and jump into the water without life-vests --- so which will it be?

If we must start all over again, the first key step is to know where we are going, because where we are going is more important than how much money we have to start with.

Leadership must now start to teach the children compassion, if they are going to be the eventual stewards of the nation's wealth. By teaching them how to be responsible now, the Nigerian children will know what to do with the wealth when it is their turn to get it or else they will turn out to be squander maniacs instead of investment oriented.

Throwing more money at problems usually creates more problems than it solves. But by involving our children in the wealth-building process (rather than consumption of wealth) at the outset, Nigerian leaders will be more apt to reach the people's goal. By doing these, leadership must chose the correct solutions to the correct problems. Leadership must determinate what the people's objectives are. Leadership must decide how much money, time and effort that must be invested to achieve the people's desired goals. Picking an objective, utilizing resources and devising several alternative plans are the keys to success. Leaders must use the people's resources to maximize the people's goals. Leadership must be clear in their objectives --- the doers versus the dreamers -- as a leader which are you?

Knowledge and education are the shortest distance between wealth and poverty. As a leader if you do not have the most potent prescription --- knowledge/education, you must seek it. In today's world, knowledge is multiplying and changing at the speed of light. Most educational testbook are obsolete before publication date --- we now have a situation where the country and its leadership are disseminating potato chip knowledge for a computer chip society. What does a Nigerian child learn during his or her whole educational experience about becoming wealthy and keeping the wealth instead of squarndering the wealth after achieving the status of wealth? Does the Nigerian child learn how to become more creative in the process of seeking and achieving wealth? Does the Nigerian child learn to devise solutions to changing problems? Does the Nigerian child learn how to create long-term wealth or just plainly, how to obtain the proper credentials from high school and unviversities to get a job? Essential understanding to the Nigerian economy and how it works is painfully not present in any form in Nigerian educational system.

Where and when will the Nigerian child learn about the free market system? About the ultimate right to fail and start

191

all over again? the need for sacrifice and individual responsibility? The Nigerian child must not equate capitalism with greed, self-reliance with selfisness and profit with cynical pillage.

If the Nigerian leadership thinks that education/knowledge is expensive, look at what ignorance has brought to the nation. Nigerian leadership steps over Naira to pick up Kobo. Many a prudent, Kobo-watching leader has decided to remain ignorant, hence, in order to save a few Naira they say no to wealth, leaders step over thousands of Naira to pick up a few Kobos because they are content with the old ways of doing things and the same old people.

Power play in Nigeria, involves money, tribe, politics and the military. The Moshood Kashimawo Olawale Abiola election debacle has exposed the country's fault lines ---- between rich and poor, North and South, Christians and Muslim. The Nigerian people are praying with hope not fear that the leadership would unite the entire country and give everyone the same opportunity, freedom and liberty.

PRINCIPLES OF SUCCESSFUL LEADERSHIP

1. Human beings can alter their lives by altering their attitudes of mind.

2. You are what you think.

3. Your aspirations are your possibilities.

4. The secret of success in life is for you to be ready for your opportunity when it comes.

5. Do unto others as you would have them do unto you.

6. All virtue lies in individual action, in inward energy, in self-determination.

7. Nothing in the world can take the place of persistence. Persistence and determination alone are the keys to success.

8. Every adversity has the potent seed of an equivalent benefit.

9. One great, strong, compassionate, unselfish person in every community can profoundly redeem the community, the country and the world.

10. History records the deeds and successes of people with objectives and true sense of direction. Oblivion is the clear position of small people overwhelmed and exasperated by obstacles.

11. Industry, thrift and self-control must be sought because they create wealth and character.

12. Progress always involves risk.

13. One person with courage makes a majority.

14. Knowing without doing is clearly ignorance. To know is to do and achieve. To know and not do is not yet to know.

15. Winners in life constantly think in terms of I Can, I will and I Am. Losers concentrate their thoughts on what they should have or would have done or what they can not do.

16. Wealth is when small efforts produce big results. Poverty is when big efforts produce small results.

17. It is not the critic that counts, the credit belongs to the person who is actually in the arena, the person whose face is marred by dust and sweat and blood; the person who strives valiantly again and again; the person who err and comes short again and again; the person who knows the great enthusiasm, the great devotions, the person who spends time in worthy cause, the person who at the end knows the triumph of high achievement and who at worst, knows that failure is an essential process for success and knows the thrills of victory and the agony of defeat.

18. Do not compete, create. Find out what everyone else is doing and then do not do it.

19. If money is your hope for independence you will never have it. The only real security that a person can have in this world is a strong reserve of knowledge, experience and ability.

20. There is no security in this world there is only opportunity --- and the usage of this opportunity separates the rich and the poor.

21. Goals are as essential to success as air is to life.

22. A person can get everything in life that they want, if they will only help enough other people to get what they want.

23. Some people have thousands of reasons why they can not do what they want to do in life, when all they need is one reason why they can ----- look around you.

24. The person who does not work for the love of work but only for the love of money is not likely to make money nor to find much fun in life.

25. Always let Almighty GOD/ALLAH to be the guide in all your endeavors --- with GOD all things are possible.

It is about time for Nigerians to come together as one nation, not a divided nation. Both North and South we need each other to make it.

People must understand, sometimes you do things that do not necessarily represent immediate gratification. The oneness of Nigeria must transcend ethnic lines. The social and historical significance of Nigerians coming together as one is the best for Nigeria.

The monumental fact that one out of every five Africans is a Nigerian, should be a thing of pride for Nigerians and increase their role to ensure that Nigeria becomes a good example to other Africans.

For decades, instead of brotherly/sisterly love to exist in the country, there is credible evidence that points to political killings and death squads being run by members of government.

Economic activity and employment have suffered enormously in the country. Recently, due to the exchange rate, devaluation of the Naira and lack of prudent management of the economy by the federal government and its leaders, the living standard of most Nigerians have suffered. The government and its leaders must take measures within the tight budgetary margins of the country to alleviate the burden of the adjustment on the poorest segments of the population.

The long-term policies of the federal government and its leaders should be directed towards generating employment and sustainable growth in the economy. One of the key elements to achieve this should be a strategy that will be focused on the promotion of exports and the strengthening and encouragement of domestic savings.

Export growth remains the important factor to the recovery of the economy. To achieve the level of investment and growth that the economy needs while simultaneously reducing the dependence on foreign financing, the federal government must enhance export growth potential at every level.

The economic programs that the federal government must put in place, must endeavor to correct the imbalances that were observed years ago, and this strategy must also ascertain that the policy will avoid the recurrence of similar episodes of economic imbalance.

The strategy that is adopted must avoid the financial collapse that has threatened the nation for quite some time. Accomplishing these lofty goals will bring a durable recovery of economic and employment activity.

I am confident that with compassionate leadership, the worst is behind us and I am compelled to note that Nigeria's future is bright. Prompt economic recovery is on sight. There are three important areas of the economy in which progress should be particularly pronounced:
1. inflation,   2. interest rates and   3. Nigeria's trade balance.

The privatization of government-owned companies and activities   --- which includes, natural gas, petrochemicals, telecommunications, rail-roads and airports will definitely fuel the revitalization of the entire economy.

The international business and finance community must

continue to see Nigeria as one of the world's most attractive options for investment.

The problems that are rattling Nigeria is transitory. The people of Nigeria and the leaders must demonstrate strength and commitment for the nation's future. Nigeria possess strength through diversification of the economy not through reliance on the oil sector alone.

The incentives that Nigeria has to offer foreign investors must stem from the recognition that a free and open economic environment -- including the strongest possible encouragement to the private sector initiative and potential, provides the best prospects for development and prosperity.

The federal government, through diversification must realize that the country can not and must not place excessive reliance on an asset (oil) of uncertain quantity and value that would not support the pace and scale of long-term growth and development of which the federal government must be committed.

The extent of the transition of Nigeria's economy away from its dependence on the primary production of oil must be reflected in its contribution to the nation's Gross National Product (GDP). Nigeria, should therefor, enter an era of economic dynamism based on a program of diversification and private sector initiative in which oil resources should become less critical or a crucial factor.

Tourism should be a promising area for diversification of the economy of Nigeria. Human resources should be at the forefront of government policy. This should be reflected in the provision of education, housing and above all health services.

Nigerian citizens should be adaptable, outgoing and computer-literate so as to be well-positioned for today's highly competitive global economy. Nigeria needs a developed industrial and financial infrastructure -- including modern transportation systems, advanced digital telecommunication systems and adequate electricity.

The federal government must put in place, economic policies that will encourage private sector investment -- both foreign and domestic, in other to build the nation's strength in human resources and infrastructure.

Although, the country is divided by ethnic politics and hatred, but the oneness in economic suffering is shown almost everywhere. Nigerian must come together as one and be strong at home first before venturing abroad.

Nigerian's made-in-USA mess --- the devaluation of the Naira, the Washington-based IMF (International Monetary Fund) imposed the implementation of the devaluation of the Naira -- partly due to Nigerian leaders mismanagement and part due to Washington's interest in controlling the world's economy.

The devaluation of the Naira that directly brought the collapse of the Naira has plunged Nigeria into a knee-deep recession that is punishing the poor people of Nigeria and has brought excruciating pain to the entire people of Nigeria.

Nigeria has slide from prosperity to poverty, everyone hopes and pray that through compassionate and strong leadership Nigeria will bounce back to prosperity and remain in prosperity.

Southerners and civilians in the country have become a relatively powerless minority in a dominant Northern/military majority that has arrogated power to themselves.

The Northerners in Nigeria are the most politically organized, rich and powerful people in Nigeria.

Members of the Nigerian Armed forces must become soldiers with a different mission -- a mission to see that every one in Nigeria has a shelter, food and employment that is paid enough to take care of a family.

Nigerian soldiers must be in service to the people not service against the people. Nigerian soldiers must fight for a new Nigeria to give hope to the people of Nigeria. The government must take as their key -- the well-being of all the Nigerian people not just the well-being of only those Nigerians who can afford the so-called good life. The maximum example of a human being's good life should be -- discipline, sacrifice, collective work for the good of mankind and a modest life-style.

The Armed forces in the country must ensure that the Nigerian people take precedence over wealth. Every Nigerian does not have to live in a mansion, but every Nigerian has the right to a shelter, every Nigerian do not have to eat chicken but every Nigerian has to eat.

The nation's leaders must form a vision for Nigeria's future. Every sane leader in the country must fight against injustice and oppression. The only thing that is necessary for evil to prevail anywhere is for good people to sit idle and do nothing. There is no wrong that can not be righted. Stand up and be counted, make a difference today not tomorrow.

There is nothing bad in the country that can not be changed into good. The good people of Nigeria has incredible energy, persistence and optimism. Nigerians are not daunted by the overwhelming economic odds facing them.

How good and pleasant it will be some day, when the North and South, military and civilians sit together as brothers and sisters and live together in <u>unity</u>. The Nigerian people are the future of Nigeria, without the people there is no country. Nigerians -- North, South, military and civilians must harness their differences for the good of the country and come together as <u>one</u>.

PATRIOTIC NIGERIANS

Past leaders have destroyed the economic and social foundations of Nigeria and they have also destroyed into shreds, the spiritual and moral foundations of the country. The nation is in so much decay, one would think she is still under colonial leaders -- who felt they have nothing to gain in the development of Nigeria, instead, so-called, born and patriotic Nigerians have been ruling the country since independence, (in one of the most blessed nations on earth) yet, bad leadership has brought the country to the ground.

Highly educated specialists are being discarded, practically the entire country is in opposition to military leadership except, the few who have something to gain from the military leadership.

People who impart knowledge for the future generations that will lead the country --- teachers, have not been paid in months, sometimes a year, yet leadership is busy building mansions for themselves -- they have no compassion. Where is the moral value of this so-called patriotic Nigerians?

I fear for a great catastrophe in Nigeria, unless leaders put their house in order. The only way out is honest democratic leadership, which will result in a moderate, responsible, professional government able to rid the country of the consequences of the hate, tribal and brutal leadership that the country has continued to witness.

The nation needs strong and compassionate leadership to restore the economy, provide social guarantees to people who can not survive without them, give young people the opportunity of a normal life/normal education and enable all talented people in the country (regardless of ethnic background) to their potential. The main agenda should be to restore law and order, human rights and the power of the people.

Repression and expropriation must stop. Patriotism is love of one's country and people. How can leaders call themselves patriots and yet unleash hatred on the same people they are suppose to serve and lead, how can patriots bring their nation into economic collapse, how can these so-called patriots continue to kill/harm innocent citizens?

Nigerians must be able to live as dignified individuals in and outside the country and feel they are part of a great nation. Past leaders can not truly call themselves patriots, because it is clear, the way they rule the nation, that they did not love their country -Nigeria, look at what they have done to the country. Since independence, there has been lawlessness and chaos. Tens of thousands have been killed, terrorism is spreading through-out the entire country. Ninety-six percent of the population is impoverished. Children are dying, hospitals and clinics have no medicine, electricity does not function adequately, yet, the government has money to spend on weapons for the military -- who is the country at war with --- except her own citizens.

The country is on the threshold of an explosion. There is poverty everywhere amidst the wealth of the nation. Stability requires real democracy, which ultimately, means that, everyone has equal rights and responsibilities under the law. The economic policy of the nation should be a combination of government-set priorities -- in housing, food, health, science/technology and culture --and provide corporation/individual initiative.

I am, as an individual, categorically opposed to any form of radicalism. I believe in the due process of law and democracy. The country must start producing products for its citizens and the country must stop being a consumer nation and become a producing nation. For Nigeria to get off her knees of economic woes and revive, the people of Nigeria must be owners and masters of their destiny.

Good leadership must have the ability of honest effort and good intentions to end poverty in Nigeria. Good government with the aid of compassionate leadership must have the fundamental confidence -- that the problem of poverty would be confronted, comprehended and conquered. In the name of optimism and to create a better society, slums must be cleared and parks built.

The military must stop fighting its brave guerilla war against the unarmed people of Nigeria. The country need a quiet revolution -- a transformation from a vulnerable, persecuted tribal society to an open, self-confident nation, ruled by moral values. A new era of coalition politics, compromise and power sharing, will signal the beginning of a quiet revolution that arises from decades of authoritarian rule to democracy.

The military in the country has been brutally suppressing its citizens for decades. The leadership must resolutely clear the legacy of historic wrongs, without political/economic revenge. In atonement, past leaders must make a monumental change and give back millions of Naira as donations to worthy programs, especially to foundations and re-building of the health-care system in the country. Past leaders will be remembered as the gatekeepers who let the cows out of the gate, because they did not prepare the country and the people for the inevitable rainy day. The people must vow to restore Nigeria to leadership with investments and reinvigorated leaders.

Leaders or individuals with great amount of money should leave great monuments in the society, just like Andrew Carnegie left the United States of America with Libraries and the Ford and Rockefellers left their foundations. Monuments like these above, help the nation and its citizens enormously. To uplift your fellow human being is a fundamental moral thing to do and it will help bridge the great growing divide between the haves and the have-nots.

Contemporary Nigeria is a nightmare where Northern Nigerians have been granted protected status, ethnic and religious privileges govern access to jobs, training programs, promotions and universities. Ethnic quotas (federal character) is being employed by federal agencies to compel employers to change their hiring policies. Naked ethnic preferences is the order of the day. Institutionalized ethnic favoritism has become the norm in private industry and in federal government policy. Using ethnicity as a category in the distribution of wealth and political appointments is disgusting. This favoritism is exacerbating ethnic tensions.

The destinies of both the North and the South in Nigeria are indissolubly linked together and the interests of both require that the federal government should not permit the seeds of ethnic hate to be planted under the sanction of any leader.

Southerners are far more likely than Northerners to be denied access to key resources on the basis of their ethnic background. Nigerians are willing to have a secure future but they are not ready to sacrifice security today, because of the uncertainties of the future, Nigerians must be aggressive in their investments more than they are comfortable with. Personal responsibility or the lack thereof, is what is behind Nigeria's sour mood. Leaders refuse to be personally responsible or accountable for their mistakes.

204

The Nigerian society and the economy is still beset by chaos and uncertainty. The nation has become an unruly oligarchy --- a power structure of rival clans made up of prominent politicians and their military counterparts --but the military it seems have gained an upper hand. The military as always is aiming to be the country's dominant power.

The Nigerian National Petroleum Corporation (N.N.P.C.), critics charge that it is growing too powerful. It is reported that N.N.P.C. in collaboration with government officials, is holding back from the people of Nigeria, billions of dollars earned from Nigeria's oil reserves just when the country desperately needs the revenues. Shrouded in secrecy, N.N.P.C. is beyond the reach of Nigerians and beholden only to any government in power ---- (AGIP). Anybody who comes to power in Nigeria has to manage to live with N.N.P.C. because without N.N.P.C. they will not manage to live at all.

The government amongst other things, must use earnings from N.N.P.C. to invest in banking, shipping, agriculture etc. Farms should be owned by N.N.P.C. to supply fresh food to its workers and sell the surplus to the general public, N.N.P.C. should also invest and help build houses, schools and hospitals. People who live in the region where oil is produced and transported must and should benefit from these wealth of opportunity. For example, based on the profit of oil sale, Royal Dutch/Shell group is the richest in the world with astonishing profits of $6.2 billion yearly. Shell group and other oil companies should and must help the region where oil is produced in Nigeria, with infrastructures, agriculture, education and general upliftment of the community and its citizens.

Legends do not just show up fully formed -- they are built layer by layer by the media and the public. Like a pearl, they begin with a grain of sand that over time is refined and grows to change the life of the individual. Thomas Edison and Henry Ford of the United States of America, were examples of this phenomenon. At the peak of their lives, each gave America and the world a picture of what America and the world wanted to be. Thomas Edison promised America and the world an era with gadgets that could make life easier, he was a man that could conquer the darkness of light with electricity and bridge distances with communications technologies. Henry Ford did not invent the automobile, but he understood the human passion for the automobile. Henry Ford put the dream of owning a car within reach of millions of people. Where are the Henry Fords and Thomas Edison of Nigeria? They are there somewhere just waiting to be encouraged by the federal government, private industry and individuals.

Nigeria as a nation, is so engrossed in crime and scandal so much so, that, if you are traveling outside the country and brandish the Nigerian passport to any immigration or custom official, the first thing that comes to their mind, is that they have a potential criminal on the scene, it does not matter if you are old or young, a Ph.D. holder or a priest or imam, but, on the other hand, a U.S.A. passport is so compelling, that it is the most official document on earth, a document so sovereign, a mere driver's license pales besides it, this instrument of identity (United States of America passport) is so formidable it transcends political jurisdictions, it is looked at with awe and it is accepted by potentates and bureaucrats all over the world.

The nation state of Nigeria is pervaded by a sense of tense uncertainty. The leadership of the country must revive for Nigeria to thrive.

We must build the rural areas and ensure that people in

the rural areas get equity in the developments. In the process of developing the rural areas, the government must not just provide adequate housing, — the government must also provide jobs, opportunities for educational enhancement, coordinate after-school recreation activities and show the people how to build a compassionate community.

Millions and billions of Naira are generated in the communities (especially in oil-producing states) in the rural areas, but less than 1 percent of that money stays in the rural areas. Most of the money goes to the military for the purchase of guns to facilitate the killings of the people from this same communities. The government must find a way to make Nigeria's money work for the people not against the people. The country and its rural areas must be re-born and re-built both physically and spiritually.

The military, in each coup announcements, claim that they want to uplift the life of the poor masses -- a revolution of some sort, but a revolution usually is for the help of the people at the bottom, but the military's so-called revolution is attacks on the poor people --- um, what a strange revolution. Leaders must find solution to the problems in the country instead of generating confrontation.

Far more demoralizing is that, I have come to see a profound loss of faith by the Nigerian people in the federal government system. Nigerians have grown unusually distrustful of the federal government and its leaders. Any nation where cynicism toward government and its leaders prevails can not function effectively.

A vacuum can not exist in international affairs. Wherever one nation pulls back, another nation will certainly move in. Nigeria has abdicated its position of power in international affairs, hence South Africa has stepped into that position.

South Africa is expanding its influence in sub-Saharan Africa. The ideal balance will be difficult to establish as long as there is a fundamental imbalance between Africa's two heavyweights; rich, potent, ascendant South Africa and a poor emaciated, turbulent Nigeria.

South Africa is now in the club of nations but Nigeria is snubbed by nations all around the world. Economically, Nigeria and South Africa have ~very high expectations of each other and both nations must consider themselves as natural partners for the prosperity of the entire African continent.

For now, Nigerian influence in the international community is declining rapidly as South African wealth becomes ever more omnipresent. Nigeria's strategy now, must be, to postpone competition of influence in the international community as long as possible until the country puts its economic house in order.

South Africa has conquered Africa on the basis of its economy, the big question is will South Africa be an African partner for progress the way Nigeria was before her depletion in the continent.

Many Nigerians are concerned about crime, and the Nigerian Police Force (NPF) is on the front lines of the battle against crime and criminals, but the Nigerian Police Force must re-examine their code of ethics -- to protect and serve --- and they must ask themselves the questions -- are we actually protecting and serving the citizens?

The people say they need Police protection and recruitment of more police officers, the people favor more manpower for police patrols etc. to reduce crime but it seems the people and the government do not want to pay more for these services.

Police salary is unjust. Police salaries are just too low -- especially considering that they are putting their lives on the line everyday.

The care for human life and human existence and not the destruction of human life should be the priority of good government anywhere in the world.

The morality of most of the Southern leaders is shaped and restricted by their primordial drives. Their capacity for rectitude and goodness exists only, so long as it serves their evolutionary interests or career development. The Moshood Abiola-Sanni Abacha confrontation has failed to produce a definitive account of what really happened between these two individuals. I hope some day we will get the clear picture. The goal of leaders should be that of promoting group/community development not just individual development.

The two major institutions that are not dealing with nation-building are the church and the mosque. It still fascinates me to note that I am yet to see any prominence from the church or the mosque in alleviating suffering in the country.

Churches and mosques must inspire the people to action through both words and deeds. Every church and mosque in the country should at least start a program where they place one suffering family with one church or mosque to educate, uplift and empower the suffering family --- at least through one child in the family.

The church and mosque must also fight crime and corruption. It is imperative and a moral responsibility that these institutions help in nation-building.

There can be no peace in Nigeria, no security, no faith in the federal government, no investor confidence and no prosperity until the crime wave is stopped and transition of government is done by ballots and not by bullets. The chances remain reasonably good for tranquil and amicable ethnic relations, North and South must make concessions to and with each other, the compelling need for compromise is now not later.

Crime prevention in Nigeria is virtually non-existent. The fastest booming industry is crime. It has infested the nation ---- corruption in government, enormous business frauds, widespread armed robbery, car theft racket and most disturbing -- whole-sale murder. Most of the victims are not Northerners but Southerners. South-on-South crime is increasing astronomically. Proper policing has been almost impossible. The people are at the mercy of criminals, especially armed robbers. The contempt for law and order left by years of grand theft-killings and destruction of properties, threatens the whole Nigerian society, corruption has spread like cancer in the entire country.

The economy is also plagued by a proliferation of strikes for more pay. The government must admit it can not finance everything. Individuals and businesses must assist the government.

The greatest tragedy of tribalism is its gigantic waste of time and energy, had all that been used to unite and advance Nigeria's people, how mighty a country Nigeria would be today.

The federal government is neither federal or united, it is an uneasy partnership bonded by mutual suspicion, the southerner is in the cabinet only to appease Northern ambition.

Real power is in the hands of the Northerners, as the nation is fast discovering, but in using this power, Northerners reveal serious administrative and financial inexperience. The handling of political and economic crisis has been ham-handed and inconsistent. Decisions are made arbitrarily. Almost everyday produces fresh revelations of massive self-enrichment at the expense of the poor masses. Administration officials are corrupt, wasteful and blatant about it.

The poor masses watch the lavish spree of corrupt administration officials with growing cynicism. Nigerians (North or South) bear the primary responsibility for making their lives better.

Some Muslim fundamentalists and some Christian extremists believe that it is impossible for Northern and Southern Nigerians to live in peace together, each believe that their people would be better off fighting to the end, to eliminate or dominate the other.

Nigerians must choose -- will their future be built on quality leadership or more of the same dictatorial leadership without tolerance. Nigerian leaders have driven the bus of economic prosperity right up to the edge of a cliff and the country is closer to going over the cliff, unless there is transition of leadership through the ballot not the bullets.

Some Southerners are insistent that only war could brake the country into North and South and bring sanity to the people and the country. These same Southerners, I hope they did not forget the Biafran civil war. The Biafra civil war was not just~ secession war of monumental collisions between the

211

federal troops and the Biafra rebels; of greater moments for ordinary people, it was a state of siege for soldiers and civilians alike, one that touched virtually everybody. The Igbo's witnessed what it was like to live for so long in such a situation, to have one's existence permanently altered by the destructive power and demoralizing forces of war.

Before the civil war, the east was a pleasant place for the Igbos, its economy was commerce,-- which included industry, banks and transportation etc. It had a lot of Igbos of great wealth and many Igbos of modest prosperity. During and immediately after the civil war, confiscation (abandoned property syndrome), indiscriminate destruction and intimidation from which very few Igbos were exempt albeit imperfectly so. After that, it was hard for Igbos to proceed with life as usual, they were clinging to any fragment of their old world, such fragments that existed were mostly in disrepair, and mere survival was the best that most Igbos could hope for.

The relative peace and calm in the country today and the emergence of prosperity once again in the Igbo community is a welcome break from the dislocations and carnage of war. All the above has caused the Igbos to loathe war.

The demon of destruction, roused mainly by a spirit of resentment, prompted the best of men and women to deeds of pillage and plunder during the Nigerian civil war and devastation was everywhere in the east. The Igbos however hung on, very well, awaiting the end of the war and the opportunity to rebuild. The war ended and Igbos have now rebuild, do you now expect the Igbos to plunge into another war based on ethnic hatred that will cause another massive devastation? I do not think so.

North and Southern Nigerians continue to wonder: what

unites us? The people seek new identity to fill the military vacuum. Nigerian lives are still earnestly redolent of the past. The people can not seem to get a foot-hold in the present economic circumstances and they do not even know what the future holds. Their expectations after decades of hardship are merely to survive.

The economic reforms of recent years are excruciatingly painful. The country is still in the grips of a collective identity crisis, still disoriented and above all, confused as an entity. Surveys show most Nigerians think their main problem in life (apart from economic doldrums) is not knowing what will happen tomorrow, even the next hour --- due to the soja go soja come mentality. Instability has also brought a lack of understanding that can unite the North and South into one beautiful country --- Nigeria (one of the most blessed nations on earth).

The horrendous psychosis in the leadership of the country is that it is all too often and all too much about the leader, not enough principle, not enough about the public, not about doing good for the people of Nigeria and not about elevating the people as a nation.

We have leaders in the country, that are hell-bent on settling old scores with real or imagined enemies, leaders that are hateful, leaders that only speak the language of vengeance. In retrospect, most people have concluded that Nigeria has had the wrong people in leadership positions, these people were not suited for the office of Head-of-state/Presidency. It is not just their criminality, their insularity, their almost total absence of a higher purpose; it is the sheer inadequacy of these people in leadership, who could not order their own life, much more the life of the nation. Leadership personality is about the organization of inner conflicts, not the resolution of inner conflicts.

213

Leadership must ensure peace and economic prosperity for Nigerians both at home and abroad now and in the future. The great passion about the pains of the past must now be focused on the gains of the present and the future. A leader must be firm, friendly and flexible. Dissention must not mean division.

The North and the South must argue but must not hate each other. Southerners must not equate delay with defeat. The People must send a very clear message, that any one who justifies, rationalizes or excuses violence as a profound legitimate part of the political process, should and must not be in a leadership position in Nigeria.

For decades, Nigerians have lived together -- sometimes uneasily, usually in peace, but always with some sense of separate identity and misconceptions. Tolerance is supposed to be the federal policy, enshrined in the flag -- unity and faith --- and must be enforced by leadership and the leadership must practice what it preaches -- i.e. show good example.

Political deprivation has deepened the pain of Southern elites in the political process. This deprivation has caused a tremendous exodus abroad of the Southern elites and those who reject ethnic-based leadership. Most Southerners --- doctors, lawyers, engineers, journalists, business men and women etc. left homes with dishwashers to wash dishes abroad to earn a living.

Nigerians envisaged a revolution in consciousness that would destroy the Nigerian system which is characterized by disorder, corruption, crime, poverty, alienation and total environmental destruction. This destructive system of ethnic based political power is responsible for the degradation of work, growing income inequality and the existence of a class of poor masses, which is the direct consequence of an economy and leadership which commits millions of Nigerians to the status of the unwanted, unused, exiled and discarded.

In Nigeria, crime rose as the economy sagged and together these two forces have stripped Nigeria of most urban amenities. Survivors of the economic doom must also confront a history of ethnic hatred that has been brewed for decades. Whether a new government of Nigerians bent on vengeance grows out of the ethnic hatred should be the long-term test of able and compassionate leadership. If political passions can be calmed by compromise and compassionate leadership, economic revival would rebuild the old wounds of ethnic trust and togetherness.

Leaders must find the courage to look truth in the eye. The overwhelming majority of the Nigerian population are dissatisfied and disillusioned with the economic reforms in the country, not because the people are obstinate enemies of economic reform but because they, like other people anywhere in the world, want prosperity and jobs today not tomorrow. The people of Nigeria can not understand the sense of economic reforms that gives them nothing but poverty, uncertainty and a high crime rate without limit.

In the years since economic reform began, the mortality rate has exceeded the birth rate. The people are cynical about leadership, the leaders have lost touch with simple Nigerians by appearing to support injustice, that is by supporting rapid economic reforms at any price and sacrificing the national interest and moral values.

For many Nigerians, patriotism signifies a simple truth; the right to decide and defend their own faith, to implement their own political/economic reforms based on their own experience, traditions and compassion.

215

Leaders must not over-emphasize ethnic problem in Nigeria and insist on special preference for some ethnic groups in the country, for example, some leaders, openly embrace xenophobia and ethnic prejudice.

The fact that patriotic and nationalistic ideas and moral values are dominant in Nigeria today more than ever before, does not mean that Nigerians are ready to renounce their freedom/democratic principles in order for the Nigerian state to thrive.

The marginalization of the Ijaws and the needs of Southerners needs to be addressed urgently towards a united Nigeria. The best and only solution to this outrage is through dialogue and not through violence or any coercive process. Government can not continue to perpetuate injustice and fight a war with the poor un-armed masses, instead, government should make a profound effort to address the problems of the poor people.   .

Mounting prosperity in Nigeria will benefit Africa and foreign investments far more than harm them because the explosive growth of Nigerian economy will present firms in Africa and the world with extraordinary opportunities, both for sales and investments. Black Africa's most populous nation will outline the exponential growth in demand for household goods and durables that will accompany the rise in Nigerian incomes.

One of the important lesson that Nigeria and Nigerians must not fail to learn is that --- sometimes you may have to take a fall to take a stand. You have to lose to win. No pain no gain.

Nigerians are facing two irreconcilable emotions -ecstasy and loathing -- have beset this fun-loving country with

216

prospective return of democracy. The military and some Northerners loathe the return to democracy while civilians and most Southerners are in ecstasy to see democracy as the rule of the day.

For Nigerians, the future confronts the past, hence most people in the country do not know if they are going or coming, a dilemma that they face on a daily basis. Once, Nigeria was invincible now Nigeria is invisible. The nation is in a quandary of crime, corruption and a collapsed economy.

It is only with a solemn mind that I can write about the prevailing conditions surrounding the poor masses of Nigeria. The country is in a state of prolonged angst, which, in effect shows no sign of abating soon unless the country gets a leader with compassion and purpose.

The reasons for this gloom in the country are many, some are very obvious but others are very much subtle. There is very little reason, for example, in celebrating a nation, in which conspicuous destruction and exploitation of human beings occur on a daily basis.

The nation is beset with problems that leaves little room for joy, ethnic relations are ludicrous, crime is almost out of control and poverty abounds. A sense of common purpose, a feeling that North and South we can work together as Nigerians in pursuit of the common good or to overcome adversity no longer exists. We have become a fragmented, notoriously peripatetic population whose roots are often defined only by how much money you have. North and South together we must build a better tomorrow for Nigeria and Nigerians.

Leaders, like any other citizen, do not know what will

work in the economic/political spectrum, they are confused and unable to steer the ship of nation-hood with a clear, concise and constant vision. The country is drowning on the treacherous shoals of contemporary times.

An intellectual degenerative virus has infected our federal system and the mantra --- dare to be great -- is now perceived as -- accept mediocrity -- , therefore, it is not surprising that there is shortage of ideas to solve our pertinent problems.

The political policy the government continue to have, is a work in progress and only time will tell if it is a work of progress. The fundamental question is whether these political policies abandon the broad national purpose of reducing poverty in Nigeria?

Patriotic Nigerians should and must challenge foreign companies in Nigeria to bring technology that benefits their home-country into their host-country --- Nigeria, for example, Siemens should bring solar technology to Nigeria.

Government corruption and a new class of millionaires and powerful criminal Mafias has emerged in sharp contrast with the ever-expanding poverty underclass in Nigeria. Nigerians must now choose to look toward the future rather than debate the past. Nigerians must also know that the deeper mystery of the North and the South thinking is shaping the country today and in the future.

Patriotic Nigerians must also know that the generosity of the United States of America is overwhelming, every nation on earth should learn from the U.S.A. and take a cue. Patriotic Nigerians must also realize that transition of governments in Nigeria should be by ballots not by bullets.

Since the oil-boom days and presently, the Nigerian

government spends too much money without saving for the future, the country is vastly inefficient and is knee-deep in debt. Politically, the country limps along. Nigeria's long-running political crisis, -- with its detrimental effect on the value of the currency is also bringing the nation into economic ruins.

Redistribution of wealth must be implemented. The economic growth should not continue to be only at the top, it must trickle down to the bottom. A sound agricultural and commercial economy must be created. The North and South must stop their in-fighting and extend the olive branch to each other, this will bring relative peace in the country and help the government to concentrate on its primary agenda --- economic recovery.

The nation is now almost immune to the insidiously creeping moral, social, political and intellectual decay. No longer do we construct pantheons to entomb famous and significant achievers; instead we dream and plan to build structures to hold events that offer instant gratification, --- (like stadiums, national theater etc.) not challenge or remind us of our highest goal and aspirations. It is very obvious that as we hurl toward the next century, the nation is devoid of myths and heroes, there are no icons or events to celebrate and unify the population. Leadership has somehow, managed to pull the people and everything apart and now they do not know how to put the people and everything together. It is Deja Vu all over again.

Perhaps it is an awakening of our dormant sense and lack of inventions, but when Nigeria's junior soccer team (the golden eaglets) won the world cup in 1985, Nigerians came together as one in celebrating this intrepid deed. People of all ethnic groups, both sexes and every economic class marveled at their strength, courage and sense of purpose in their

219

accomplishment. Since then, there has been very few~ (if any at all) national celebrations that brought the entire nation as one. Most unifying events has been funerals. It is indeed overwhelmingly sad and a depressing mark on our national psyche, that we are only united over death, we came together bewailing a tragedy, a fallen leader (for example: Awolowo and Aminu Kano's death). Perhaps it is time to celebrate and promote success. Human infirmity become irrelevant as epic heroes are born. Nigeria needs heroes today and now.

TRIBALISM

When people fail to win the Presidency, they should help redirect the political dialogue in useful ways, an example is Ross Perot of the United States of America, by an extreme contrast, politicians who lose Presidential elections in Nigeria continue to rebuild the field upon which Nigerian politics is played, making ethnic malice, fear and tribalism the central issue out of which virtually all other issues grow.

Tribalism, thanks in large measure to one or two politicians in the North and South is the nation's consuming political obsession. These Presidential candidates, for all their subsequent rhetoric about empowering the poor, -- ethnic hatred was the foundation upon which their political career was constructed. Whatever, Nigeria's other short-coming, we are a forgiving people, hence I would call on all Nigerians to forgive these politicians.

The ethnic hatred being spread by these politicians were committed in a spirit of self-interest that is so mercenary and cynical as to defy comprehension. The tribalism groundswell that transformed Nigerian politics in the 1990's began with these politicians in the 1960's. In truth, these politicians have never believed in anything except the political and financial advancement of themselves. They also left Nigerians with a legacy of division and hatred. Most Nigerians know their history but not their future.

To build something that lasts, it takes hardworking people, it takes people with vision, it takes people who care. In today's Nigeria, doing nothing is not an option we should live with. We must all wake up and do something, something positive in every little way.

Leaders must know that domestic politics is the heart of successful foreign policy. A leader must also be a fascinating media wrangler. A leader must also know that before you can succeed abroad, you have to know how to survive at home.

There are so many minefields and heartaches of tribalism in Nigeria. In the country, it is still the case, that people tend to see your ethnicity before your capability.

Leaders must be careful with words, because words that are not used properly will create a climate of intolerance and might lead to unnecessary violent uprising.

With the unpredictable and highly competitive economic/political environment, leaders with vision are desperately needed in the country.

Although, government is best when it governs least, but the collective sense is that the federal government has the responsibility for the health, education and welfare of all its citizens.

As a nation, we have not learned to talk frankly (due to fear of persecution) and to listen carefully across ethnic lines. The ultimate proof is that one can do well by doing good. We, as Nigerians must all shoot for the moon but if we mis, at least we will be among the stars.

The government is retrenching workers (Southerners) and turning them into criminals, think about it, what are you suppose to do when you can not feed your family through legitimate work? You look for alternatives.

It is not weapons but words and will that makes dreams come true, because after all is said and done, what is a legacy?-- it is just another word for love, and what Nigerians must know is that learning is a lifelong process, learning does not stop after you graduate from the university.

Nigerians must believe in the power of new ideas and a new generation of compassionate leadership. We, as Nigerians must respond to the changing of times -- with strong vision, values and a sense of purpose. Nigerians, in private business or in public service in federal/state and local government must ensure that job performance is primary but the people are paramount. Nigeria's future must be defined and refined.

When the core of leadership is based on performance, nothing will be more important than the performers, absolutely nothing. We can not change Nigeria's past but by God's grace and compassionate leadership, we can take control of Nigeria's future. Strong and compassionate leadership must show the people of Nigeria what to expect tomorrow today.

The rules of engagement in the society of Nigeria must include -- excellence, innovation and compassion. These will help Nigeria take a quantum leap into the future with economic prosperity.

The world operates because lots of individuals do individual things. People should start doing instead of talking. We need the value of cooperation instead of competition. One would assume that it is easy for soldiers to change from war to peace because they have been on the battlefield and they know the smell of blood and they also know that it is not good to spill innocent blood especially when there is no war.

The nation needs religious and ethnic tolerance and it takes every one to achieve this, not just the government alone, because plain people can change Nigeria, the prophet Muhammad in the Koran was a merchant not a government official, Abraham in the Bible, was a simple shepherd not a government official.

Leaders must bring disparate people together to emphasize points of commonality rather than points of division. Nigerians have to be aware that Presidential politics is about personality not necessarily policy. People must also realize that leaders will say and do anything to stay in power.

The federal government (either under military or political leadership) must not believe in the censorship of speech they find incorrect or disagreeable and must not be utterly intolerant of dissent.

Most Nigerians are better at describing the problems in Nigeria than they are at prescribing its cure. Now, in Nigeria, cruelty is as natural amongst the people as fresh air is to the country. Maybe cruelty is the oil that powers the political engine of bad leadership.

What is it about Nigerian leadership, that makes them so unreceptive to the pain that is felt by the people? Evil continues to exist in Nigeria because both the federal government and the rich elite in the country has turned their backs to the poor people of Nigeria. In Southern Nigeria, greed is the potent oil that fuels Southern retrogression.

Alarmed by the increasing numbers of the poverty class and disillusioned by corrupt politicians and corrupt military officers, Nigerians are currently looking for moral leadership. The Nigerian poverty-class are destitute and desperate in the land of plenty ---- Nigeria.

Everyone tries to shift blame on the other, but no one is

coming up with concrete everlasting solutions --politicians blame the military, the military blames the politicians, we have an almost endless game of blaming one another.

Nigeria is beset by repeated bloody coup attempts. Nigeria's long record of coups, plots and power struggles does not inspire much faith in a by-the-book transfer of power. The questions surrounding the transfer of power should be resolved by political intrigues and not by uprisings and shooting one another on the streets of Lagos or Abuja.

A broad redistribution of resources must be enacted to provide electricity, water, roads and housing to rural areas.

Since the oil-boom days to present day Nigeria, the country has had a dream deferred, because during the oil-boom days, the government said the country has so much money they do not know how to spend it. If you have so much money and do not know what to do with it, the logical best thing to do is to save it for future not squander all your riches and then return to poverty status. After squandering an enormous amount of wealth, the country is now playing catch-up.

The big difference that compassionate leadership will bring, is that money should start flowing into Nigeria instead of flowing out.

In politics, you find out how difficult it can be sometimes, to quickly translate campaign promises into governing reality when unexpected diversions come right and left.

Nigerians, with all the resources the country has, must now move from company workers to company owner; the goal should not be creating separate tribal societies but rather a diverse society in which every Nigerian succeeds, Nigeria's goal should be interactive and integrated.

Nigerians are the biggest technology consumers in Africa. Nigerians must recognize that somebody had to invent these things -- T.V., satellite dish, stereo, C.D. players, videos etc. Most Nigerians can tell you the names of sports stars, but how many of them can tell you the name of the scientist who invented the compact disc? We should encourage our children to be interested in science and technology.

The average Nigerian should be fiscally conservative but socially progressive. We must manage our dwindling water resources through conservation and reuse and also build more dams.

Most Nigerians have no ideas for planning for the future, they can not see five years down the road, they are too busy trying to get through the next day, hence, it is insurmountable to think about next month, much more think about next year or next five years.

If you are surprised about what you see now in Nigeria, you will be astounded about what you see next in the future if leadership is not compassionate. The federal government under compassionate leadership, must make hard work, self-reliance, individual initiative and merit --not just membership, i.e. federal character, the basis for success in Nigeria.

The people of Nigeria are clearly fed up with the lack of moral rectitude among public servants. Guaranteed satisfaction in public service is what the people are looking for.

Federal government of Nigeria, -- federal -- means the government of Nigeria is stable, trustworthy and omnipotent, but reality has shown, that the federal government is neither stable, trustworthy nor omnipotent.

As I have said over and over again, due to intermarriages (between North and South) at some time in the next century, a majority of the country will be people of mixed ethnic group without a clear, defined or distinct tribe. The time is now for Presidential power sharing arrangement between the different ethnic communities of Nigeria.

Many Nigerians openly criticize government policies in conversations on the streets and drinking spots (beer parlors). But spoken criticism between individuals are one thing, putting complaints down in writing in the media or distributing them for a wider audience amounts to subversion in Nigeria and it is harshly punished. There are people in government who think you can not allow information to be freely available. These government officials do not realize that a lot of issues are really economic and political and changing Nigeria is through good leadership.

Wealthy parents must know that special privileges insulate children from the real world; these special privileges gives the children the illusion they do not have to play active roles in planning for their futures. A significant number of children from wealthy homes are literally, socially handicap by the process of special privileges. Impatience, dependence and arrogance, these are the characteristics nurtured by the special privileges environment.

Present day leadership are a creature of the past not the future. Nigeria needs leadership for the future not the past. The future of Nigeria is in jeopardy because of past misdeeds by bad leadership. Nigeria needs compassionate leadership that is committed to change. Leadership must be open to dissent, flexible and constantly searching for new ideas and

227

options.

The poor masses make up a potent constituency in Nigeria where apathy and disgust with leadership reign. The fault of the economic down-ward trend is blamed on bad leadership. The fish (as they say) rots from the head not the tail, hence it is the leadership of the country that needs change not the poor masses. Hope, sacrifice, courage and working together, that is what will make Nigeria great. We must replace fear with hope, -- disease with health, --- and confusion with direction. If you think the past is scary, the future is positively terrifying, unless we work together in unity as one Nigeria (North and South).

Nigerians must answer the question of whether we will be able to go forward together (North and South) as a unified society with a confident outlook towards the future or as a society of diverse economic groups suspicious of both the future and each other.

The unambiguous conclusion presently, is that economic rewards in Nigeria are distributed unequally. The poor and the working class have seen their wages decline over the last decade, while the middle class has stagnated and the rich continue to grow wealthy. In the early 70's however, what seemed to distinguish winners from losers was how much education you had, but now, education has nothing to do with wealth in Nigeria.

Taken one by one, many of the country's problems today are simply examples of poverty breeding poverty -problems that are in most cases solvable, however, years of mismanagement and the federal/state government viewed as the employer and investor of first and last resort have produced a bureaucracy that is not conditioned to reward efficiency.

Leadership must not be concerned with ideological debate over whether to bring economic prosperity and political stability to the nation, leadership should just do it.

In Abuja, a city born of and built by politics, the reaction to complex problems that are inherent in Nigeria is often not to resolve them but to manipulate them for political advantage by the leadership in power. Niger state ceded land to create Abuja city. This is supposed to be a special place, the nation's place, a city for every Nigerian, and therefore should neither be affiliated with a state nor be a state in its own right, but contrary to its creators, Abuja is fast becoming a city for Northerners and by Northerners. The North and South must realize that neither can do much without the other's consent, that consent must be won and trusted.

Like partners in a struggling marriage, their roles ill-defined and the balance of power ever-shifting, the North and the South have never come to terms with each other. They distrust each other too much to cooperate; but they need each other too much to declare a total breach.

Some other problems continue to elude the power of the federal government --- urban demographics continue to work against the federal government, rural residents continue fleeing to the cities leaving the farms unattended, skilled professionals (especially private business men/women) continue fleeing to the U.S.A., Europe and other African nations. The nation is left with a population increasingly dependent on the federal/state government for support.

During the economic boom of the 1970's, the federal government and the entire leadership spent money as if the era's robust economic growth rate would continue forever, it did not, economic doom hit; denial set in. Leaders later conceded that they ignored reports that the country was going broke. Spend-thrift leadership and mismanagement so gross has brought the economy on its knees.

For the North and South, working together offers intriguing potentials. Both North and South must appreciate that the depth and complexity of the nation's problems require a new sense of partnership -- the kind of partnership that will bring about radical but cautious and practical change for the prosperity of Nigeria.

Due to bad leadership, Nigeria is missing an opportunity of epic proportions in economic transformation. If history has shown the world one thing, it is that economic growth takes place when trade barriers are removed. The federal government must remove trade restrictions to allow economic growth to thrive in Nigeria, this will create jobs, strengthen Nigerian businesses, bolster Nigerian exports of goods and services and improve the economy tremendously. Exports of goods and services plays an increasingly crucial role in the economy of virtually every nation, export of goods and services play the most potent role in the economic growth of Nigeria.

Leaders must demand more from themselves to bring Nigeria forward in the realization of economic prosperity and political stability. Like a soccer team that has won a national or world championship cup for a very demanding coach, leaders must find their pleasure in what they have accomplished (the cup) not what it took out of them (hard work). By any standards, this should be an era of extraordinarily large change for leaders to lead by good example, this should orchestrate the realization of a vision of change to good leadership and a nightmare to the pessimists.

Nigeria and Nigerians must choose between visions of the future versus politics of the past. The nation needs more substance over symbolism and function over form. It is not the package but what is in the package. Leaders of this century must put the future and good of Nigeria first and self last.

Faith makes you a leader, -- courage, vision and the will to succeed makes you a hero. As a leader, you have to fight hard for your principles, but you have to fight smart. You do not just lash out and fight just for the fun of fighting. There are ways that you can pursue your goals quietly. What matters is not the fun of the battle but the result of the battle, not how you win but who won.

Leadership is the ability to solve problems not create problems like people do in Nigeria. Freedom comes with a fight hence you must fight for your freedom, this fight must not mean taking the life of another human being. Things you need for success as a leader, 1. safety first, 2. look before you leap, 3. risk is worth the reward, 4. do not panic, 5. if you can not beat them join them, 6. no pain no gain and 7. plan ahead.

The balance of life for a leader, believe, achieve and succeed, you should see possibilities instead of limits, you should turn your vision into reality.

To be paralyzed by the hostilities and conflicts of the past or to be comfortable with the status quo in the interest of peace, -- a profound compromise with each fundamental scenario is what some people believe will ensure peace and hope for the country.

Compassion is the potent way that we can transcend the turmoil, the blame game, the needless pain and misunderstanding that ethnic differences often trigger and move on to a much sweeter and more satisfying pursuit;

prosperity for every Nigerian (period).

As a leader you must carry your riches in your person and be ready to generously share who you are not merely what you have, because what you have can disappear overnight but who you are will endure for a lifetime. Leaders must ensure that contemporary politics is freed from the age-old linkage to religion and vice versa. I am convinced that politics and government meddling with religion produces intolerance, persecution and bloodshed. Zealous pursuit of religious opinions, far from leading people to cooperate for their own common good often leads them to irritate and harass each other. Leaders must insist that their religious views or anybody's religious views are not political issues.

Time and again in Nigeria's history, its leaders have always opted for physical beauty -- monuments, federal buildings, office buildings etc. -- over social justice and compassion for the people of Nigeria. The obvious result is the country today,; a place full of some huge buildings but increasingly polarized along ethnic and class lines, with a dwindling population and economic disparity.

In reconstruction of Nigeria after the civil war, physical improvements took precedence over social engineering. In most countries, issues transcend ethnicity, but in Nigeria, ethnicity more often transcends issues.

The future looks better when you start planning for it today, hence Nigerian leaders and the people of Nigeria must start planning for the future of Nigeria today not tomorrow. What is good for the North is also good for the South, vice versa.

As a leader, you must show the country and the people what direction they should be heading, the country and the people have been drifting for a long time, it is now time for bold leadership to show the true path to progress. There is no time like the present time. Failing to prepare means preparing to fail. Demand extends to leadership. Leaders must not only demand sacrifice from the people, but leaders must also sacrifice for the people.

Leaders must have passion for their profession. To lead, you must lead by example, good example and not bad example. Nigeria will progress through compassionate leadership. The federal government and its leaders must finance tomorrow's needs of the people with today's income. The future is bright but leaders must invest in the future today. Leaders must save for a rewarding future today. The dark crimes of bad leadership of the past will and must come back to haunt the perpetrators. A country is judged not by its accomplishments alone, but by its compassion and the welfare of its citizens.

The country must achieve a history of growth, prosperity and innovation. Leaders must put the possibilities of the future with-in reach. Leaders must stress commitment to quality stewardship and success. Leaders must pursue the challenges of tomorrow with today's commitment for success.

Leaders and the people of Nigeria must have the vision to see change as opportunity. Today's leaders face exciting challenges but the only well-traveled road is the path of leadership. Bold leadership with compassion are the potent partners on the fast track to Nigeria's prosperity. It is your future, hence you must stay ahead of your future, with the right people in leadership positions anything is possible especially good things. Nigeria must seek leaders who are problem solvers with a crystal clear view for the past, the present and the future. Good leadership will make Nigeria's view of the future crystal clear. Shaping the future of Nigeria

233

starts today not tomorrow.

Compassionate leadership will bring fundamental changes that will insist on power-sharing between the North and the South which will lead Nigeria into a peaceful and progressive country, a country with more jobs and less <u>crime and better human rights guaranteed for every citizen of Nigeria</u>.

When people can understand that through power-sharing everybody can get a slice of the pie, even if it is not a big slice, everything works better. This will cut out the inherent and continuous hatred in the society. But there are a lot of Nigerians including myself who are too dignified to hate. I am just too busy to hate. We need an atmosphere of tremendous cohesion for unity and discipline. Many people have come to the conclusion that Southerners have no hesitation voting for a Northerner in an election, but Northerners they claim, have reservations about voting for a Southerner.

SOLUTION

In seeking practical solutions to the nation's catalog of problems, the leaders must consider cost effective factors in problem solving and decision making. Leaders have been known to find themselves often preparing a solution before the problem is thoroughly analyzed. As a result, poor ineffective solutions can be time consuming, costly and often demoralizing to the leaders and the people, who must continue a concerted effort to deal with improperly resolved problems. Two facets of problem solving skills are <u>reasoning and creativity</u>. As with any skill, the development of reasoning and creativity requires time and patience. The search for solutions into the country's problems is now not later. No debate on solving Nigeria's problems is complete without the development of an action sequence designed to avoid future foreseeable undesired outcomes. Most people know or are familiar with the adage "prevention is better than cure".

Many leaders do not know when a problem begins, because, what they often neglect to do is to set measurable standards. Only if leaders set standards and follow the same standards as prescribed to the people, then everyone can be sure to recognize a problem at the proper time. We only have a problem when we get a result we do not expect.

Nigerians do not expect the result they have now in their economic and political bondage, hence, we need leaders that lead by example and set measurable standards for people to see good results not bad results.

There are two very distinct parts to any problem solving sequence and they are 1. problem analysis and 2. final and effective solutions. A clear line must be drawn between the analysis of Nigeria's economic/political problem and the ultimate search for solutions with the emphasis clearly on thorough analysis of the problems.

Leaders must ensure that the solutions eliminate the problems for good, because it will be questionable if solutions were put in place yet the problems keep reoccurring over and over again. The solution process might be slow and painful in the beginning but it will speed up as time goes on and it will be less painful. Leaders must also understand that a partial solution that shows only some desired results is absolutely no substitution for a full scale solution.

Nigerians everywhere must cooperate with good leadership to achieve the proper solutions for Nigeria's problems. It is very advantageous for Nigerians to choose leaders who are problem-solvers not problem-creators as we have seen in the past, I can not stress it enough to go to our heads, we need leaders with compassion, compassion, compassion and compassion.

To find out the cause of Nigeria's problems, an effective leader must get down to the details -- to principles that were immensely violated, one of the principles that were clearly violated that resulted in these economic/political problems confronting the nation, is the ability to find leaders who care about the well-being of the entire nation instead of the ethnic area where the leader came from or caring only about his or her immediate family's well-being.

The position where past and almost present leaders have put Nigeria and Nigerians is a travesty. The trend of poor leadership in the country has been overwhelming. Something drastic in leadership overhaul is needed immediately to bring Nigeria back to her days of glory.

The fundamental phenomenon of resistance to change must be put in perspective when analyzing problems and bringing up solutions to the economic and political problems of the country.

One must put into consideration what change means for the people on the receiving end, the people in one hand and the leaders on the other hand. Their concerns must be appreciated, because invariably, it means a change in the behaviors of the people and the leaders. Every person one way or the other tries to circumvent change because in reality, change is unknown from the normal routine of one's behavior, but essentially, change is good, change is very good.

Time, economic reality, adequate information and leadership by example, all these have to be regarded when bringing up solutions to Nigeria's problems. It takes time, money and effort to stop a bad trend of leadership.

We need leaders that will stop Nigeria's problems -i.e. eradicate them, because like in normal human life, one is cured from acute headache when the doctor's prescription stops the excruciating pain not when the doctor's prescription makes the pain bearable, hence the nation needs solutions to stop the economic and political problems not to make them bearable.

The ultimate goal is future prevention because prevention is better than cure and knowledge is power, knowledge is the key to any cure and prevention. knowledge is a potent medicine.

The people of Nigeria and their able leaders must not be discouraged at any stage if early applications of the prescribed solutions are time-consuming, because time is required for solutions to mature and accomplish the set objectives of the solutions.

Care, fundamental principles and expertise must be used to avoid future economic and political problems. The ultimate value of a leader is his or her ability to solve problems and evade future occurrence of problems.

Political change is being resisted at all cost by the old brigade of Northerners but the contemporary Northerners are not only ready for change they are also ready to share political power with Southerners.

Rather than see Southerners complain about their political positions and the so-called unfairness, the challenge for Southerners is for them to use their advantage on education to overcome the political positions they find themselves in.

Nigeria must be moved from being an impoverished nation to an economic giant. In recent years, the people of Nigeria have been accustomed to an era of constantly changing governments through military coups and a federalism system based on patronage and expansive military spending to satisfy the appetites of the military elite. While Christians dominate the South and the federal civil service, Muslims dominate the North and the military might.

The constant political crisis in the nation is a total reflection of a desire for change in the political structure. Also the incessant military coups in the country is wiping out the glimmer of optimism that prevailed decades ago in the economic arena.

Leaders must make political decisions not based on personal gains but based on the future of the country and gains for the country. All through the oil-boom era and now the oil-gloom days, Southerners have instilled in themselves self-hate that is propelling them towards self-destruction. For decades now, South-South homicide has been the leading cause of death for Southern Nigerians. The cynicism, corruption, dishonesty and power abuses by Southerners against each other should be more of an immediate and future concern.

Seeking fundamental political change is inevitable but this must not be confused with the enormous task of self improvement and compassion by Southerners for Southerners and the entire nation. People must continue to ask the question ---- who is really a threat to the Southern community --- the Northerner or the Southerners themselves? The desire for .Southerners to blame the Northerners for political backlash has continued to generate more enthusiasm among Southerners instead for every Nigerian to have a concerted effort to build up the nation socially, economically, humanly and politically.

Governments all over the world are suppose to exist to protect individuals in exercise of their rights to life, liberty, property and justice, but this is not the case in Nigeria. Nigerian governments as of late has existed to kill the rights to life, liberty, property and justice for poor individuals. Individual freedom can only be protected by a federal government that is actively concerned for the welfare of its citizens.

Power usually comes from the personality of the man in office. Presidential power is the power to persuade the people to do the right thing not power to kill people for alleged coup plotting and all other excuses to justify homicide. A President or Head-of-state should be the voice of the people not the voice of the military or political party, a national leader not a military or political party leader, protector of the peace for every Nigerian not a chosen few and above all a leader, President or Head-of-state should be a manager of prosperity for all.

Myriad of interests (economic, ethnic, social and religion) have an enormous stake in maintaining the dispersion of governmental power made possible through federalism.

If Nigerians want the country to bounce back to the antecedents of economic prosperity, the leaders and the citizens must insist on adequate and efficient power supply so as to compel foreign companies to invest in the country. American companies want to invest in Nigeria but most of them complain of the electricity scarcity and lack of government stability.

Nigerians, due to lack of patience, must also realize that, the nation and past governments have made more mistakes in haste than gain opportunities in delays. Nigeria thus far has become a society striving to have order in the midst of so much chaos.

Leaders must inform the people that everything in the nation should be based on community, cooperation and compassion. Leaders must also be aware that the logical consequence of the abuse of power is the loss of that power. Eradication of corruption launched by a corrupt leader is not just an exercise in futility but an exercise in hypocrisy.

Politicians must realize that in order to reach the majority of the people, a leader must be especially sensitive to the particular concerns of different states in the federation. Good organization and strong leadership qualities can also make the difference between failure and success in political leadership.

I still marvel over events of war all over the world including Nigeria's civil war, (ethnic cleansing) in Bosnia,

Rwanda's civil war, Liberia's civil war and world wars I and 2, just to name a few. In all of these wars and many more, both warring factions sat on the negotiating table to accept peace after thousands if not millions of lives have been slaughtered, all in the name of war. The question is ----- if both aggrieved parties will end up on the bargaining table, why not explore the monumental phenomenon called "peace" to the fullest instead of rushing to take arms and kill each other and then end up bargaining for peaceful settlements? Like always, events, like people may continue to surprise you, but history keeps repeating itself. War usually sets a nation back at least 20 years --- roads, electricity, water facilities and housing are totally devastated after war.

I pray and hope Nigeria does not see another civil war because I believe that both North and Southern Nigerians can manage to co-exist peacefully without military confrontation if leaders can sensibly share power.

Poor Nigerians have been forced to make excruciating sacrifices over the past decade as the entire agricultural sector continue to shrink to its lowest ebb. Milk and meat have disappeared from the Nigerian diet. The collapse and restructuring of Nigerian agriculture has been followed by deepening anxiety and a monumental sense of loss.

So many Nigerians are starving, parents can not afford to feed their children, children faint in schools, it makes you wonder, probably the Nigerian leaders enjoy seeing this situation.

The cynicism that persists in the country reflects the public's frustration with obvious bad results of federal government policies. A compassionate federal government of any administration --- be it military or civilian must defend the poor person's right to government assistance.

Government must immediately solve the hunger problem facing the nation, the war on abject poverty in a wealthy nation must be won decisively and government must provide opportunity for everyone to progress regardless of ethnic or religious background, all you need is to be identified as a Nigerian and as a human being.

For decades now, the nation has been in an era of pessimism instead of optimism, an era of ultra shrinking of expectations from leaders by the people, a lot of fear, a lot of anger towards leaders who have raped the country and its treasury.

Leaders should empower the citizens and instill in them --- accountability and responsibility. Citizens have to ensure that all infrastructures, to the extent it exists and functions, should be theirs to administer, maintain and renovate, but above all, leaders must first lead by example -- i.e. good example.

When citizens are involved in the participation of governance it will reverse decades of inefficiency and mismanagement. Equal participation in government gives the people a sense of pride and belonging, but isolation of the people by leaders make the people angry and hungry for power. The moment the people are involved in governance and become masters of their own destiny, this will right the historical imbalance that have existed for decades between the leaders and the people.

The federal government must adhere to long-term development plan for the entire nation. For every rural area, there should be long-term development plan for roads, airports, seaports, water facilities, electrical plants, hospitals and schools. I wonder how rural areas without these infrastructures have continued to thrive and exist for so long.

A leader must not only have able advisers but the leader must have the ability to use the advisers effectively. Complaints around the country is that General Ibrahim Badamasi Babangida attracted able advisers but he regularly ignored their advice and kept his advisers in ignorance of several key decisions and chose to run his administration alone.

In contrast, people assert that General Yakubu Gowon demonstrated an ability to use advice effectively, keeping control of key decisions and effectively delegating power. It has often be inferred that General Gowon has the ability to know his limitations and most of the knowledge to draw on the brains of other people.

A strong leader must have the ability to unite the various ethnic groups in the nation. The nation is divided by geographic, ethnic, religion and ideological factions, but must be skillfully united by the President or Head-of-state.

The gap between proposing change and implementing it is wide but must be bridged by strong leadership. A President or Head-of-state must assure the various interests, groups, ethnics and leaders in the entire nation that he will be President or Head-of-state of all Nigerians not a section of Nigeria. The President or Head-of-state must also heal factional wounds created during crisis. A President or Head-of-state must realize that opposition is unavoidable between a chief-of-state who wants his policies reported favorably in the media and the media whose ultimate job it is to question the chief-of-state's policies. This is an inherent conflict that must be managed properly by both branches (the media and the Presidency).

One of the inherent use of the media by the President or Head-of-state is a clear fact that success depends on invoking the role of national spokesman and leader. The President or Head-of-state can not be perceived as a party partisan or military partisan because if he is perceived in a partisan light it will lead to public disillusionment and cynicism. The anxieties of political crisis brings a yearning from the public for the Presidency to be occupied by a non-partisan leader.

A responsible and compassionate leader must get public feedbacks and use these feedbacks either as a guide for policy planning/implementation or as a guide to reach the people. A President or Head-of-state must not be perceived by the public as rigid, unresponsive to public demands or defensive on issues that inevitably will affect the entire country.

The widespread national awareness of the existence of political crisis in the country, calls for change and are clamoring in all spheres of life, people are demanding leadership by action through co-existence not domination by one ethnic or religious group.

Political offices must be shared by both North and South, Christian and Muslims. Most of the riots and killings in the country are expressions of discontent over the sluggish progress toward inequality in political office sharing. A strong leader must provide assurance to the public that the country belongs to all Nigerians and bring about policies that will include all Nigerians involvement in governance.

One way to revamp the Nigerian economy is for both federal and state governments to accelerate spending on goods and services such as schools, roads, hospitals, dams and electricity. Increased government spending on these infrastructures will start an economic spiral for the good of the nation, instead of buying luxury cars for traditional rulers and military officers as gifts.

245

The nation is faced with unprecedented unemployment and banks that are closing or crashing on a monthly basis. In other to put people back to work the federal and state governments must embark on a great policy of spending that will provide jobs for the people. Economic recovery should be paramount in the minds of the leaders, while pumping Naira into the economy. The government should direct the Nairas to areas that would stimulate enormous economic activity and have a huge social impact. Economic expansion to the poor is long overdue not just expanding the wallets of the rich few in the nation.

A leader can define issues and set terms of debates but no leader can dictate the outcome of issues and debates. Instead of creating jobs to halt inflation and massive unemployment/economic disaster, the government lay-off workers and delay payments of salaries to the so-called lucky few that have jobs. Families are devastated because parents can no longer afford to feed their children.

For decades, each succeeding administration had greatly underestimated the enormous rise in unemployment. Workers were laid-off due to tightening economic policies. There were also the natural increase in unemployment due to retirement of military personnel especially Southerners.

Economic initiative must come from the chief-of-state to lower inflation. Companies will have to lower prices through increased industrial productivity. The goal of the federal and state governments including the private sector should be a massive effort aimed at creating more jobs.

For a great Nigeria in health, education and welfare, the country needs jobs, jobs, jobs, and jobs not a continued government concern with proliferation of trials of alleged coup plotters.

The government should be concerned with the rapid rise of prices in consumer products and the continued growth of unemployment which gives rise to armed robbery, fraud, hired assassins and even collapse of human compassion.

All through the economic crisis that the nation is faced with, the leaders personal economic prescriptions have continued to run counter to public expectations. Government economic programs (due to incessant change of governments) has been through with inconsistencies, also the economic and political preference of the public continues to be in conflict with the people in power.

The federal government must create more jobs, stop the ultra high cost of living from rising any further and protect the Naira from relentless attacks on the international money market. Government must encourage business investment in machinery and equipment and assist the agricultural industry. The skyrocketing cost of health care must be eliminated totally.

For decades, it has been obvious, that soaring food prices, especially beef and rice, were not temporary catastrophes, yet the government has not done anything to alleviate this health hazards ---- food shortages thrive in every corner.

Food prices has continued to rise, inflation has not been controlled effectively, corporate profit margins continue to increase without re-investing in the economy. Governments are expected to take strong action to deal with economic crisis, but Nigerian government economic track record for decades has been very dismal.

Until the end of the 1970's, Nigeria enjoyed an enormous surplus of, exports over imports. Military coups, coupled with the economic and political crisis has caused other countries to lose faith in Nigeria. To revamp the economy requires careful planning, just like in agriculture, if the ploughing, planting and tending have not been successful, there would not be any harvest. Government must place emphasis on the use of science and technology to improve the lives of Nigerians.

The military and its personnel must improve the lives of Nigerians, the military is meant to defend Nigeria and her territories, not instead to put the country in a continued emergency position. The military is in a better position to make a great difference to the society by being compassionate in peaceful times. The nation must use science and technology to meet economic and social needs.

Development of natural resources, water supplies, electricity, mass transportation and public health, these require the adequate use of science and technology.

Any President or Head-of-state that excludes the public from decision-making has ultimately decreased the people's stake in supporting his policies. Presidents or Head-of-state in recent times have isolated themselves from the great mass of Nigerian people especially the youth of Nigeria, thereby contributing greatly to revolt and continued protest by the youth toward the government.

The only national figure and national spokesman that the nation looks up to with concerns of crime, business, agriculture etc. is the President or Head-of-state. He is responsible not only for his own actions and decisions but for everything done by every Nigerian hence he must lead by showing good example.

A chief-of-state must not be denied contact with reality and deprived the chance to learn from his mistakes if he is willing to learn, because most Nigerian leaders think that they are not privy to make mistakes while in reality no one is above mistakes. Every chief-of-state should enter office with an asset of novelty and hope for the country.

Most Nigerian leaders do not fulfill their promises to the people hence disillusionment sets in and the result is further isolation. Only leaders with the capacity to use flexible sources of information (not only the reliance on official governmental sources of information) to his advantage will minimize the impact of isolation. The interest of the leader must be connected with the interest of the people. A leader must coordinate the nations past and the nations future to merge in prosperity. The chief-of-state must be forward-looking geared to innovation. The chief-of-state must also allow the media to assist him in investigating waste, corruption and wrong-doings in the federal government. Every criticism in the media about the government should not be seen as a confrontation between the government and the media instead it should be seen as a way for government to correct its mistakes.

Despite their inherent rivalry and differences, cooperation is possible between North and South, because, they are mutually dependent on each other to coexist. Both North and South must work out accords and build bridges to bridge the gap between them.

The military, instead of having confrontations with the media, should be-friend the media and build a strong public relations image of efficiency and public service. The military should provide military personnel, equipment and expert technical advice to assist the nation in every area, this will no doubt enhance public support for the military. The support will be so compelling the military will be lost for words. The public can not afford to be hostile to a military establishment whose main weapon is public service and not self-enrichment. The military must care for the people, ---- people whose lives have been devastated, people whose lives have been shattered, people who have no hope and people who are poor. The military corps of engineers can assist in building of roads and irrigation projects for farmers.

Nigeria needs a leader who is strong, who has ideas on how to solve problems ---- especially economic and political problems. A leader with a consistent sense of direction and sensitive in the poor's ordeal to survive and prosper. A leader that will be able to provide bold, imaginative, decisive and durable solutions to the economic and political crisis in the nation.

The chief-of-state and the Nigerian people should have the willingness to respond to the economic and political crisis in an imaginative process. A leader that would enter the office of the Presidency determined to meet the challenge the office offers with tough-mind pragmatism based on flexible approaches and realistic assessment of the national situation.

The leader must also emphasize helping the poor to strengthen their independence through economic, political and social progress. A leader that will implement the assistance of the poor through national development programs. A strong, leader must find a way in the conflicts between the people's survival and military spending under peaceful times. This must be resolved quickly.

The nation must reduce the pace and dimension of rearmament for the military in the interest of the economic crisis. Nigerian leaders must choose between guns and butter, butter for the people or guns for the military. The nation must cut military spending to provide resources for national development programs. Do not misunderstand this scenario, because it is true every nation prefers a strong military establishment, but you can not continue military spending when the people can barely survive.

The cost of military preparedness is rising more rapidly than the economy, hence government must cut military spending and increase spending on social and development programs. It is obvious that any leader with the guts to propose such changes will run into conflict between the military and the people --- in the long run such a leader will be loved by the people but will be hated by the military, but if the leader sets its priorities effectively, he will ultimately be loved by both the military and the entire nation.

The military must maintain an enormous public relations department geared to promoting a good image with the general public, not continuous scenes of military brutality against civilians, instead the nation should see the military co-existing with civilians in a compassionate atmosphere.

The tragedy of the economic disaster is not simple theory of evil men inclined on a conquest for personal aggradisment or supreme honor, instead, it is the devastation of an entire generation.

CHANGE

Prudent planning makes you realize that nobody lives forever, hence you must have contingency plan for succession of leadership. Glory and guts not glitz and glamour are the potent means of prosperity. One of the greatest strengths that America possess is the potent embrace of "change". Nigeria must and should be willing to change.

It is not how fast you can go, it is where you can go. A wise man will change but a fool will remain the same. We need less debate but more decisions.

Instead of seeing the strength and compassion of leadership, Nigerians continue to see the cruelty of leadership. Leaders must swallow their pride and share power and hope for the best for Nigeria's future.

Past leaders and their cronies have used the treasury as their personal bank account instead of the treasury belonging to the people of Nigeria.

The federal government should be a partner with the people not against the people in working for the welfare of the people of Nigeria.

The road not taken for Nigeria is the Abiola Presidency. This is the wistful regret for the nation's missed opportunity in an Abiola-led administration. Nigeria must take the lead with a path into economic prosperity and the future in Africa.

As a leader, you must have a vision beyond politics, you must aim for Nigeria's economic prosperity and keep your focus on compassion.

You must be proud of the past and respond to change for your future. You must have a commitment to help others help themselves.

Nigerians must be reminded of the courage that is often required to speak out their minds, this message is especially appropriate for a nation where so many people have been cowed into silence because of fear of persecution. Leaders must have a commitment to learn and discover. A leader's job is to show Nigerians the future ------ bright or bleak.

The future of Nigeria's children is an open book ---- open a book with the children and let them get an education. If you can not manage your time you can not manage your life.

Most of the oil produced in Nigeria comes from Rivers state yet there is no single oil company that has its headquarter in Rivers state, they are all headquartered with large skyscraper buildings in Lagos state. Shell, Mobil, Texaco etc. should have their headquarters at the source where oil is produced -- Rivers state.

Leadership is not about power it is about service, it is not about power and authority it is about wanting to help people. Leaders who are power politicians are most times uneasy populists.

Economic/political independence will make Nigeria secure and ensure stability. Eventually the political/economic fight in the country will be the poor against the rich and privileged. Nigerians must have the zeal of making the most of whatever they have left.

The true meaning of success is taking less traditional paths to professional prosperity. As a leader, you are getting paid to do what you love and discover a great sense of individual satisfaction. Effective leadership is both financially rewarding and personally fulfilling. A leader and a government that has a vision can do magnificent things.

Most military administration and its leadership has been charged with what went wrong in their administrations but they have not been credited with what went right.

Nigeria must choose between guns or butter. Nigeria is a wealthy sleeping giant, it may be stirring now, but it has not yet awakened but believe me, the world will see Nigeria when it is awakened.

The world admires people who rise above adversity hence the world and the people of Nigeria will admire Nigeria if the country rises above the current economic/political adversity. The nation wants leadership that delivers ---- good not bad fortune.

The nation and its people must live within their means because if they do not, there will not be any choices left. Government is supposed to be used to enhance personal freedom for the people not private wealth for the leaders. To lead is not just giving eloquent speeches it is by providing the most potent effective leadership.

Nigerians must not be satisfied with success for success's sake and the people must not be discouraged by failure because failure can be sad but the most potent sadness is not to try and fail but to fail to try.

A leader with commitment to excellence must tell the peopie not to be afraid to walk a path that has not been already paved. Self-satisfaction is the key to happiness .

Change is the dynamic of life that we can not avoid but

we often snub change. Life itself is for growing and growth demands change because in the process of growth you inevitably change. The only way to stop growth/change is to die, hence as long as you continue to live, you must embrace change, because change enables us to open ourselves to the unforeseen which makes us develop faith, wisdom and courage. Trying to circumvent change is the source of most of our problems and unhappiness; fear, which leads to doubt and procrastination is the potent enemy that holds us back. Fear of change, lack of faith for the unforeseen makes us to cling on problems instead of looking for solutions. The difference between joy and sadness is how we embrace change and how willing we are to start all over. The key difference to happiness is the commitment to planning and change for the better. You must believe in possibilities of change and you must recognize that the possibility for change is in your hands.

One of the main reasons why children do not want to learn in schools, is because their environment is too bleak and their future looks bleak, hence there are no incentives to do anything.

In Nigeria today, loss of confidence creeps into all institutions --- especially government. Most people say if they can not trust each other, how can they trust the federal government? A lot of people are apprehensive about the federal government because it is made up of people they do not trust. This mistrust of each other is the major reason Nigerians have lost confidence in the federal government and virtually every other major national institution. Nigerians now believe that most Nigerians can not be trusted, they assert that there are too many Nigerians trying to hurt their fellow citizens financially, emotionally and physically. Decades ago, before most Nigerians became so power/money hungry, majority of Nigerians trusted one another. In essence, this collapse of trust in human nature has fueled the erosion of trust in government and virtually every other institution.

The federal government also suffers from a lack of public confidence because of other national discontents brought about by the perceived failure of the federal government's inability to deal with the nation's problems.

Fear of crime, economic insecurity and pessimism about the lives of present and future generations all have separately added to the notion that the federal government is making things worse or is generally incapable of making things better.

If trust were a trait slowly acquired over a lifetime, this might be a problem for Nigeria, trust however, is acquired in early childhood and is far more likely to diminish than to increase with age. If young Nigerians are not growing up with a sense of trust, then, there is really no hope that they will develop trust. Trust in most individuals might erode due to events or circumstances, but if you do no have trust, you do not acquire it.

Trust in the essential goodness of others translates into a rosy glow about Nigeria and its institutions. Mistrust of one another ultimately breeds suspicion toward government and most times outright fear.

An atmosphere in which an enormous proportion of Nigerians believe that most people can not be trusted in the country breeds attitudes that subsequently hold all public servants including the military as corrupt, venal and self-serving ----- and this perception also hold all federal government actions as doomed to failure.

This cynicism has made people to believe that although leaders call themselves public servants but in the real truth they are self-serving, they say one thing but do another, they do not practice what they preach.

There is also a potent conviction drawn between economic well-being and trust in others when things look bright as they did in the 1970's during the oil boom, people trusted each other, after the oil bubble bursted, now, when people worry about the future few people trust one another.

An overwhelming percentage of Nigerians see the federal government as wasteful and inefficient, they also believe that the federal government has not done anything to help Nigerians in need. The discontent over the economy and bad leadership adds to public fears about the future and the belief that prosperity will be more difficult to achieve for future generations unless there is compassionate leadership today to lead the country into a brighter tomorrow.

The media (the fourth estate) more perhaps than any other institution involved in the fashioning of public policy, is now accused of being responsible for most of the nation's problems. The press considered itself to be the protector of the public interest.

A lot of Nigerians have surveyed the journalistic landscape over the past few years and have concluded, more in anger than in sorrow, that journalists are losing the public trust by painting a gloomy picture of government and government activities.

Journalists and journalism can find the way back to public trust by embracing the essentials of the movement called public and civic journalism which stresses the value of citizen-inspired reporting instead of self-centered and self-destructing the nation's integrity on the pages of a newspaper or magazine. Public and civic journalism aims to make people feel reconnected to the public life of their government and their community -- this agenda makes journalists to take the wishes of the people into account not the wishes of the media. Such journalism will inspire and nurture a better community.

People are asking if journalists want to entertain the public or to engage the public? People also want to know do journalists want to inform or inflame the public? Right now it is not a matter of one or the other. Journalism is a complicated enough responsibility, yet the best journalists do entertain as well as engage and inform the public not inflame the public.

Some journalists, however, in an effort to sell papers and provoke unnecessary conversations have spread unsubstantiated rumors, outright lies and venom about public officials and celebrities. Obviously, hate sells and it is virtually impossible to correct the misinformation and distortions that are so easily disseminated.

Nigerians must choose between leaders with new ideas, no ideas and wrong ideas. In with the new and out with the old.

Nigeria's ruling class must have to see that nurturing the cultural infrastructure in every bit is as important to the survival of a country as its physical infrastructure. Cultural self-determination is a virtue that the ruling class of Nigeria can not afford to surrender to the western world. The ruling class must focus on the needs of the community and promote prosperity and general happiness in the country. The ruling class and its leaders must run the country with a national budget that will include a 50 percent reduction in military spending but an increase in funding for education, health care and adequate housing.

Nigerians foolishly expect the federal government to fix everything. Nigerians also demand that the federal government be everything to everybody at the same time. The federal government pretends to be so responsive to popular demands that it has almost lost much of its capacity to distinguish between what is desirable and what is do able. The federal government that is supposed to dedicate itself to happiness now breeds enormous unhappiness. Meanwhile, the media incessantly reminds the population how bad things are on a daily basis hence making people feel more vulnerable than necessary. The people have been filled with so much bad news that they now mistrust institutions and feel betrayed. The Nigerian people are tired of hearing about problems without hearing about solutions.

Without goals, priorities and planning, we are leaving the future to chance, and we are paying the price now. If we do not identify our ultimate agenda/goals we can not know which way to go -- forward or backward.

As a leader, you must create an atmosphere in which mistakes are tolerated, because, little of value is accomplished where nothing is risked and to take a risk, you must be willing to make mistakes. To succeed as a leader, you must pay attention to the future and be ready to change at any given time. The essence of being a leader is achieving objectives through the efforts of other people by delegating and giving them a vision of what must be accomplished. A leader who can not delegate can not change and can not lead. While delegating, a leader must also tell his or her people that he or she expects clear thinking from them not blind acceptance.

The nation's accelerating population loss is among the worst in Africa for this decade. But viewed over the long-term, Nigeria is simply catching up to the same grim trend that took its toll in many African countries decades ago. The nation's population is shrinking faster now than almost all other African countries.

European countries and the United States have been pulling Nigerian citizens out of the country due to better housing, better schools and an enormous growing pool of jobs. Nigeria as a nation has also pushed people out of the country because of higher crime, deteriorating public services and an enormous worsening poverty.

The trends are very alarming and daunting but my potent intuition is that Nigeria has not gone to the point where it has lost the basic resources that it could use to rebuild itself. The country has more poor people than its pre-oil boom days and the poor in the nation are more widely spread out geographically in the nation. The people in the country need more active cooperation in supplying public services and fostering employment.

A great leader is not the one who does great things, a great leader is the one who leads the people to do great things. Because of bad leadership and leadership with no compassion, Nigeria is becoming two nations ----- North and South, ---- hostile, separate and unequal.

Though, I am a religious man, I believe that only a clear separation between religion and civil authority could prevent tyranny. Religion must not be a qualification for public office. I am tired of hearing Nigerians (mostly Northerners) deny that ethnicity does not play an important role in determining life chances and career opportunities.

261

Leadership should be focused on issues not personalities. When you look at the social conditions in Nigeria, it becomes obvious that Nigerians must do more for themselves regardless of the leadership's historic failure to live up the ideals of the nation's constitution.

As a leader, you have to look back but think forward. Leadership and the people of Nigeria --- standing together ---- together a new beginning. The question is are we going to protect the old or embrace the new? We must learn from the past and effectively pay the price now before it becomes too costly later on.

WHAT LEADERSHIP MUST DO

Leadership must empower the citizens. The present and future generation of leadership must focus their attention on two priorities -- 1. educational reform and 2. economic development.

The leadership should challenge every Nigerian to commit themselves to new kinds of learning, new kinds of cooperation between the North and South, new kinds of responsibility as parents, students and members of the community.

A leader must have insight, character, devotion and modesty so as to bring warring factions into common grounds of counsel.

The truly strong leader is not the one who relies on his or her power to command, the truly strong leader is the one who recognizes his or her responsibility and accountability and knows that as a leader he or she has the opportunity to enlighten and persuade the people.

Leaders must know that, bad policies today are tomorrow's consequences. A leader must have the political will and the administrative skill to enforce <u>change</u>.

The leadership, be it military or civilian must bring itself to respect substantive differences of opinion and remain tolerant to variances from the government message on issues

Instead of leaders polarizing the South and the North they should unite them. Nigerian leaders should put human rights above property rights, they should also stop being arrogant and inaccessible. Their code of conduct should be loyalty, decency and honor. Every leader must put in place a reminder that because he or she suffered, there will be more healing, because of their grief, there will be more joy. Leaders should work for the good of others.

Feeding the hungry and housing the poor should be a priority to the federal leadership. The Nigerian leadership should set an action program to vanquish poverty and injustice. The Nigerian leadership should invest on the people of Nigeria.

The leadership of Nigeria must learn to help others while helping themselves, hence they must enjoy today with 10% (ten percent) and keep 90% (ninety percent) for the future of Nigerians.

Leadership emerges naturally when the leader attracts followers. The leader should be a teacher, a coach, a mentor, a developer of human potentials and team builder.

Leaders must take care of the people at the bottom or else the top will fall. The nation's leadership must devise a strategy to bring people of all faiths together. Leadership must give hope and encouragement.

The leadership must give equal rights to all Nigerians for equal participation in the political process regardless of their ethnic background. A leader must have moral vision.

Leadership that strives to be the best must have four c's 1. concept, 2. competence, 3. collaboration and 4. connections.

Leadership should not only have the four c's but master the four c's; 1. concept -- leaders must possess knowledge and ideas and must also continually upgrade their leadership skills, 2. competence --- leaders must be able to perform at

265

the highest pedestals, 3. collaboration -leaders must work together to address the nation's common concerns and 4. connections -- leaders must know the right people all over the country.

To achieve success in the economic and social life of Nigeria, leaders and the people in every community need to work together.

Leaders must capitalize on all the natural attributes or assets that they have. Leaders must be able to communicate clearly across cultural and or ethnic lines and leaders must possess the physical stamina to work ultra long hours.

Leaders must have an in-born commitment to helping solve the communities problems.

Leadership must address all the problems that limits growth in the society which includes high crime rates, traffic congestion in the cities of the federation and the faltering education systems around the country. Leaders must be prepared to change at any given time. If Nigeria is to achieve greatness, leaders in Nigeria must put the future of Nigerians first not last.

A leader must be a defender of the downtrodden. A leader must have solidarity with all victims of injustice. A leader in Nigeria must be aware of the inner contradictions between the past and the future of Nigeria. A leader must, at all times contemplate the future of the country.

Leaders must teach by example, the values of social order. Leaders must show the right form of civil discourse.

Leaders must know that ambition translate into achievement. Leaders must be determined and leave nothing to chance.

Leaders must have a cause they dedicate their lives to beyond their own private interests. Leaders must know that the comfort of their future life depends upon their present conduct.

Leaders in the country must take leadership roles in negotiating, compromising and working to build fences that will bring the country into one entity.

The leadership must bring confidence in the nation to restore shaken investor confidence in Nigeria.

Leaders must be free-minded and defend policies that will enable the country to achieve economic prosperity.

A good leader must be cautious, must be deeply sensitive to the ebb and flow of public opinion and must be aware that government is a process of consent and accountability.

The indispensable qualities that a leader must have are:- steadfastness in a cause, perseverance against difficulties, efficiency in the execution of policy, patience and prudence.

Every leader must act to preserve the safety of the nation. Every leader must save the nation from catastrophe.

A leader must make it his or her duty to keep close to the people. The leader must be exposed to a wide range of national opinion. A strong leader must be strong with the people not against the people.

A leader must accept the obligation of accountability and the discipline of consent. A leader must incorporate within himself or herself an array of diverse value from every ethnic group.

A leader should see a greater variety of people, consult a wide range of opinion and tap more diversified sources of knowledge.

Leaders must concern themselves with public opinions instead of only worries about their own political future.

Leaders must extend power to the Nigerian people. A strong leader must be sensitive to the diversity of concerns and opinions of the Nigerian people.

A strong leader must maintain a divergent range of contacts and surround him or herself with the most articulate and positive thinking advisers.

Leaders must make a difference. Leaders must know that equal opportunity with government assistance is a moral thing to do.

A leader must cultivate a personal relationship with the media. A leader must always be in touch with the people.

A leader must have the ability to serve as an effective shaper of public opinion. Leaders in Nigeria must end the rulership of the country by one ethnic group, one religious group, one region and self-interest.

Leaders must lead a crucial war against poverty and hunger. Leaders must not be seen as encouraging crisis instead of talking peace.

A leader must find out what the people want and give it to them. Leaders must acknowledge that North or South we are Nigerians first and foremost. We must speak with one voice in other to succeed in our collective efforts to bring sanity and prosperity in the country -- it is a difficult task but it is a task that we must all strive at and ensure the success of oneness. Leaders must lead by open-door policy with the public.

A leader must be a person who is kind and loving and cares about others, not a person who goes to church or mosque every week and look down on others because they do not live the life of a Christian or a Muslim. A leader must act by doing deeds for others.

Leaders must know that government is an instrument for creating a better society. Leadership must encourage fundamental changes to improve the long-term economic prospects of the country.

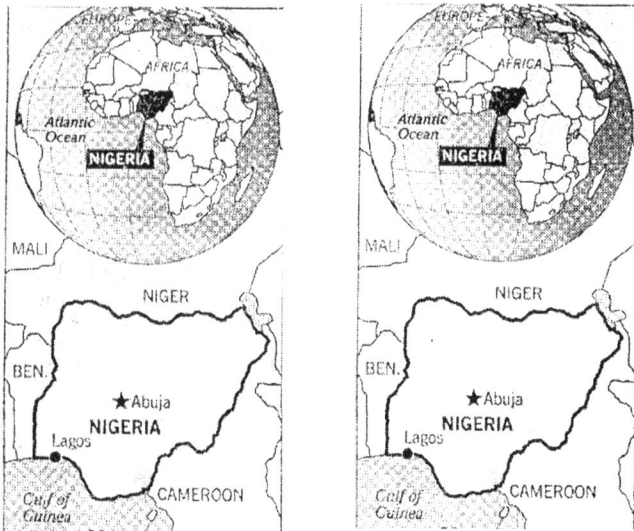

269

One thing must be made clear to Nigerians, --- as long as the poor, the young and the Southern population remain sufficiently unorganized, the Presidency or Head-of-state will continue to be a Northerner, with that, the Northerner will be unable to initiate the major economic restructuring that could alleviate the needs of the disadvantaged Southerner.

The growing energy and food crisis throughout the nation means that there is increased competition for scarce goods whose distribution the government can not dictate. Increasing food costs seems likely unless the people and the government make a concerted effort to stem the tide.

The nation continues to witness the government's inability to solve the urban, rural, ethnic, poverty and food crisis. There is now a general decline of confidence in government by the people. Declining public confidence in government is likely to affect in a spiteful circle the economic and political revamping of the country. Evil has continued to triumph in the country due to the lack of compassionate leadership.

As the nation continues to undergo violent political, social and economic change, enormous demands and huge expectations remain the focus from the people towards their leaders. The nation needs service with leadership. The nation needs a leader that has persuasive skills with authority not a dictator with commands, a leader with political sensitivity, a leader with a consistent sense of direction and a simplistic sense of proportion. The problems incurred by inept leadership in the country are magnified by the fact that the public has also lost a sense of direction. Effective federal government policies depends on the skill of the President or Head-of-state.

Leaders have failed to accomplish significant goals and as such they have cast a dark cloud to the future of the country.

270

The nation needs a leader that will create a new sense of excitement and significance about government and service to the people which will attract many able Nigerians to serve the nation.

The ultimate performance of a leader as President or Head-of-state is the expression of his or her personal preferences, needs, ethics, passion and his or her inherent ambition to succeed in strong leadership with compassionate service to the people and the will to admit mistakes and take responsibility.

A President or Head-of-state should and must be judged on the basis of his or her successful use of power to further the objective of creating a Nigeria in which the greatest possible degree of individual/collective growth and development is possible, despite religious, ethnic, military or civilian background. It is unfortunate that at several crucial moments in Nigerian history, such individuals were not available, the public hopes and continues to pray for this kind of individuals to emerge and take charge with compassionate leadership.

TO BOOK **TONY OYATEDOR** FOR SPEAKING, CONSULTING, AND WORKSHOPS, PLEASE SEND ALL INQUIRIES TO:

TONY OYATEDOR
PRESIDENT/CHIEF EXECUTIVE OFFICER

NEWSTIME FOUNDATION
PO BOX 434, RIVERDALE, MD 20737
U.S.A.

OR

NEWSTIME FOUNDATION
PO BOX 3135
FESTAC TOWN, LAGOS
NIGERIA

The objective of NEWSTIME FOUNDATION, is an attempt to spread ideas and shape the debate for A BETTER NIGERIA. It is also a medium to raise funds for "PROJECT HOPE" for the future of Nigeria -- based on AGRICULTURE. NIGERIA -- FARMS AND FOOD NOT FIST AND FIGHT. FARMS NOT ARMS. NEWSTIME FOUNDATION is a conservative THINK TANK.

The TEN DOLLAR ($10.00) CRUSADE. This is a program geared for every Nigerian diaspora and for citizens of the world that wants the betterment of Nigeria, to donate $10.00 or its equivalent or more to the NEWSTIME FOUNDATION. The funds, would be used to assist Nigeria in three major areas: 1. Food Production, 2. Electricity and 3. Health Care.

Also, proceeds from the sale of this book will be donated to General Hospitals around the country. For each book sold, part of the proceeds will be donated to OYATEDOR SCHOLARSHIP FUND to help students in need in Nigeria. The only thing that grows faster than money is TIME.

Time is growing fast on Nigeria but money is growing less.

We need leaders that will give us solutions, not excuses. I believe that if you are not part of the solution, you are part of the problem.

When you get older, you get more at peace with yourself. The fundamentals of what is important in life are: 1. Getting food on the table, 2. Keeping a roof over your head, and 3. Clothes on your back.

You have to have a vision, you have to know where you are going and you have to empower people. We should be here on earth and in Nigeria, especially, to heal not to divide. People should do little things that can have an enormous impact on big things.

Basic research -- is where scientists are free to pursue their curiosity and interrogate nature, not with a short-term, practical end in sight, but ultimately to seek knowledge for its own sake and for long-term practical end in sight. Hence parents and leaders in and out of government must encourage individuals who are driven by curiosity. Nigerians must know that the main purposes of high school (secondary school) education are: 1. Preparation for work, 2. Post-secondary education and, 3. Most of all, productive citizenship.

I (personally) know that I never race or rush but true to my name I always arrive on time, because I believe in planning. I also know that ethnicity has caused so many devastating problems for NIGERIA, but for the North and

South, our strengths far outweigh our weaknesses. It is time for Nigerians to choose the farm life over the city lights.

My biggest pit-fall about writing this book is that, I did not complete this book-- I literally abandoned it. The large part of publishing a book is that it never ends, you keep having more different thoughts at the last stages of publication, but subsequently you have to put a stop at some point and here it is.

T.O.

MR. TONY & MRS. VERONICA OYATEDOR

THE AUTHOR
TONY OYATEDOR